The Bardo Thodol
A Golden Opportunity
Transcripts from several discourses given by

Mark Griffin

The Bardo Kunda* ~ March 3, 2007
The Bardo Satsang ~ March 8, 2007
Q & A Satsang ~ October 30, 2001
Weekly Meeting ~ March 13, 2007
Q & A Satsang ~ June 22, 2008

Hard Light Center of Awakening

Kunda means "wellspring, a source of continuous supply". In the Kunda Series, meditation master Mark Griffin explains and demonstrates the nature and experience of profound subjects dealing with advanced consciousness in the human form.

The Bardo Thodol © 2008 by Mark Griffin,
Hard Light Center of Awakening
ISBN 978-0-9759020-2-8

All rights reserved. No part of this book may be reproduced in any form or by any means, electronic or mechanical, including photocopying, recording, or by any information storage and retrieval system, without the express written permission from the author.

For more information about the **Hard Light Center of Awakening** please visit *www.hardlight.org*. The web site provides a complete listing of Mark Griffin's other books and CDs, as well as links to audiobooks, podcasts and PDF books.

The **Hard Light Center of Awakening** is an organization founded and directed by Mark Griffin as a forum for the study of spirituality and meditation. Mark Griffin is a Meditation Master who is firmly established in the advanced Nirvikalpa Samadhi states — rare strands of consciousness that lead to remarkable perception and spiritual accomplishment.

First Edition: January 1, 2008
Second Edition: July 10, 2008

Transcription, Editing, Illustrating: PodPublishing

"You should understand that the greatest opportunity you will have for enlightenment, the golden ticket, is handed to you at the moment of death. Get that through your skull. It's not something that should be feared. It is a golden opportunity for enlightenment. Ninety-nine people out of one hundred who generate enlightenment do so at the moment of death."

"It's when you become very versed in the idea that life and death are the same, that the potential of the samadhi condition – which is the absorption of one's identity, the absorption of one's mind into the Great Light – while still in possession of the body, can occur. Why wait?"

Mark Duffy

TABLE OF CONTENTS

The Interval 1

The Pathway of the Transition 35

The Three Stages........................ 39

The Phowa............................. 61

The 100 Fibers of the Chonyid Bardo 79

The Sidpa Bardo 94

Illustrations / Plates 103

Questions and Answers................. 111

Q & A Satsang March 8, 2007 147

Q & A Satsang October 30, 2001 199

Weekly Meeting March 13, 2007......... 207

Q & A Satsang June 22, 2008 217

Index 231

CHAPTER 1

THE INTERVAL

Today we have the opportunity to engage in the auspicious dharma discussion of the profound subject of The Bardo of Life and Death and the interval between these two conditions called the Bardo Thodol.

The term Bardo means place or interval and Thodol means enlightens upon contact. The idea expressed is that the interval between life and death is enlightenment itself. It is the Great Light. It is the Clear Light of Reality. Contact with it is immediate enlightenment if it is recognized as such.

The text that is one of the most famous about this subject is, of course, *The Bardo Thodol*. There is also *The Egyptian Book of the Dead*. The text is divinely originated by the great enlightened personality Padmasambhava, manifesting in the 8th century. It's very interesting that he did not feel that the human race was capable of understanding the text while he was alive, so he wrote it in the 8th century and hid it in a cave in a mountain, whereupon it was discovered four centuries later, somewhere in the 12th-13th century. It has been filtering into our society ever since. The person who found the text was a fellow named Karma Lingpa. He was a denizen of the Himalayas, Northern India, and he was just a boy when he found it.

The text is a description of the architecture of the human form and its relationship to consciousness. In other words, there is an idea of a relationship between form and consciousness that arises in a form of awareness that we call 'mind'. It is an extremely subtle diagram of how consciousness moves from the formless condition of pure consciousness into mind, into formation of life force and into the formation of physical body; how it manifests as the form of life and then its deconstruction, wherein the life force-mind-consciousness matrix move through a set of conditions that are regulated by karma and karmic conditions. The quality of thought and the quality of actions bring about the trigger of the separation of the mind from the body and the absorption of mind into the Great Light, what is called 'The Clear Light of Reality'.

The Bardo of Life and the Bardo of Death are thus understood to be one thing, wherein a set of highly fluid conditions are unfolding at all times. Between the condition of embodiment – where the consciousness that supports and arises as the mind-heart-body matrix – and their deconstruction and re-absorption is the Bardo Thodol, the intermediate state, the condition between embodiment and disembodiment.

It is the totality of the ocean of consciousness, the Great Light, the infinite expression of mind in its completely unconditioned nature, and all of the mechanics of the individual existence. We understand our conditioned nature to be hinged on the assembly of memory that is assembled around the operation of the senses, organized by the intellect and apprehended by the reflex of consciousness that we call ego. This is the underlying support of the egocentric identity. It is the image of the drop of the individual that exists in the great ocean of consciousness. As consciousness moves into its embodied condition, a series of layers or sheaths buffer and condition mind, buffer and condition awareness, buffer and condition universal consciousness, and operate according to the laws of individual perception and individual experience. Thus the drop, while still being thoroughly one with the ocean, lives a dream of separation in the interval of death wherein the mind and the body are separated from each other and the mind is reabsorbed into the ocean of consciousness. It is the dynamic of death.

The interval in between is the fluid event wherein anything can happen. This is the first all-important principle that you must understand. Life and death are the same. What is most important at the moment of death is the ability to recognize what is occurring. Death, like life, is highly complex, subject to ignorance, superstition, fear, confusion and emotional affliction. As we know well in life, all of these lead to errors in judgment. We have a desire within ourselves, we are faced with a set of conditions – the desire within ourselves and the conditions come together and they somehow mix together and produce a brew. We make a choice and the choice is either the fruit of clear perception of what is going on or, more likely and more common to all of us, our desire for what we want to have happen. This greatly conditions what we perceive. In other words, we see what we want to see and our choice is not based on the reality of a situation but rather a hope. Then we make a choice and it turns out, "Oh, it was a wrong choice, we made a mistake, we made an error in judgment." We see people that have the ability to clearly and incisively understand the situation in life, make decisions accordingly, and they are more right than wrong and we see that they prosper to a certain degree. A person that continually makes errors and judgments makes the wrong choices and we see that their lives seem to be a journey from one disaster to another.

The moment of death is not the slightest bit different and in fact, it's even a little more dramatic because it's all happening at once. In life we have the effect that it seems to be spread out over a phase of time. There are moments of peace, moments of joy, moments of pain, moments of hope – the entire panoply of emotions that we are all familiar with, take place as if in a dream. If we are graced and beloved of God, we all hope that we live a long and happy life. But as we know, and as very few people are willing to admit until it's too late, death is inevitable, death is certain.

We get absorbed in the fabric of the quality and the experience of life and we think, "Well, death is far away." And we even have the capacity to produce a flurry of activity that will convince us that death is even further away. We have the strength, power and beauty of our youth; we have the involvement with our loved ones, our family and the hope of our work in our lives. And even having lived a long, full and happy life, the day of reckoning comes, the moment of death arises and the drama of the event of death unfolds very swiftly. Once struck by death, the very swift and irresistible force of the separation of the elements of your mind from your body, and the absorption of your individual being back into the ocean, does not wait. It's almost like a machine. It is this quality, like an inexorable force, that hits a program of deconstruction and you are deconstructed. Prayers for relief, prayers for expiation, prayers for release are of no avail. It is a force of nature.

Most often this event is unprepared for because we've lived a life that is designed to keep the subject of death as far away from us as possible. We don't even want to talk about it, let alone think about it. We don't even want to think about it with any depth or detail because it's frightening, something beyond us. This is superstition, this is ignorance and it's the wrong tact to take.

The spiritual proposition of yoga and the basic thesis of the Bardo Thodol is that life and death are the exact same thing. They are an arising of conditions inside the Great Light. This being so, the advice from the wise is that life should be used to prepare for the darshan, the contact with death. Everything we do in our spiritual training is training for this; yoga, meditation, the study of the breath, the listening to the SoHam, the vibration of SO, which is the mantric manifestation of the creation, the vibration of the HAM, which is the mantric manifestation of the Clear Light, the Great Light of Consciousness and the space between the breaths – the interval.

Right there is the map of the Bardo Thodol. Apparent existence – SO; infinite existence as clear light – HAM; the interval between the two – the manifest quality of the change of attention from the apparent creation to the void infinite consciousness. They arise simultaneously, but attention flickers between the two. The space between the breaths is the Thodol, the interval, where we come into direct contact with the Clear Light.

We've discussed the mechanics of this a thousand times – that the throb of the breath – the in-breath and the out-breath carry the vitality of the life force. The life force carries the mechanics of the five-fold pranas – descending energy, ascending energy, the cyclical revolutionary energy, expanding and contracting energies, and the energy of infusion. It is these five envelopes that produce the mechanics and produce the stable connection of the apparent creation.

The raising of Bodhicitta. The word *bodhi* means awakened. The word *citta* means mind. This is the direct recognition that the spontaneous nature of mind is of the nature of enlightenment. It is void of quality, of the nature of light. By generating one's will to arouse that enlightened component within one's own nature, draw it to the fore with all of one's behaviors and activities, we actively express enlightenment in a low, middling, great or profound way in our life.

I cannot stress enough the power of thought on the impact of the nature of life and on the impact of the nature of death. The quality of one's thought is the event. It's not abstract. It's not like "Oh, I'll have a bunch of thoughts here, and then I'll have another bunch of thoughts later, and these are all bad thoughts, but when the moment of death comes, I'll only have good thoughts." It's a hopeful thought, but oftentimes is not the reality. Because of the sheer ferocity of the onset of death we see fear, we see panic, we see superstitious and false understanding.

Your life and your death are the same. They mirror each other. It's as if there's a subtle dial within you and during life, the SO mantra is dominant – apparent, arising. As death begins to occur, everything starts to dissolve. You should understand that all of the components of life and death arise within your own thought-constructs. This is why everybody subtly understands that we create our own lives with the quality of our own thought and the activity of our own mind and heart.

It is because of this all-important understanding of the connection between life and death that we engage in spiritual training. We learn to meditate. Strong meditation is basically a trip between life and death – traveling in the intrinsic Bardos of our own nature.

Meditation, the study of breath, the strengthening of the vitality of the Bardos is about learning to run the energies of the five pranas in the right channel and in the left channel, and merging the vitality of the life force into the central channel. Some of you have been studying with me for some years. What is it that we're always studying? We're always pressing, getting better and better at aligning the mind, the life force and consciousness with the three central nerves, the ida, pingala and sushumna – female, male and central nerve.

The Bardo Thodol, the interval, takes place inside the 3 ½ feet from the base of the spine to the crown of the head. That's the interval. That's the Bardo Thodol. The event between life and death takes place in the left and right channel and in the central nerve between the coiled serpent at the base of the spine and the brain at the crown of the head.

There are two aspects of dharma. There is worldly dharma and holy dharma. The worldly dharma is the dynamic of the psychology, the control of one's appetites and the resistance to the six poisons of anger, greed, envy, pride, fear, and ignorance. As an act of will we filter them out of our thoughts and we filter them out of our behavior. Why? – Because if we give rise to them, we have printed jealousy into our lives. It manifests in our life as our life. We think we have the luxury while we are still alive and embodied to go, "Well, I'm just going to sit over here and have these really dark thoughts about jealousy or greed, about a certain person or condition. Nobody is really going to call me on it. I'm just going to be sitting in my room and it's going to be fine. And I'm going to crank out all of this negative energy through my system, through my heart and through my mind."

This is like drinking poison. And that poison

produces a stain in your life force. Now it's possible to expiate them by generating good deeds, but we've all heard about this idea that at the moment of death your entire life passes before you. Well, that's true, it does. And basically, your mind-heart-being is a perfect recorder. Every single thought, every single feeling, every single action is recorded. Where is it recorded? It's recorded in the central nerve and in the left and right channel as subtle samskaric bits of data. As you are going through life, you have the luxury of the phantasmagoria, "Well, tomorrow's another day." But death is a little bit different. Death tears away the filter and the buffers of personal identity and the raw energy of every thought. If a thought and an action are born of greed, then that energy of greed manifests inside your mind stream with incredible intensity, without any buffer, and you experience it as a deep poison. Same with anger, same with hatred, same with lust, same with jealousy.

If on the other hand as an act of will and wisdom, you say, "Well, I understand that these actions carry a poison that will harm my soul, and as an act of will, I will turn my heart and my actions away from fear. I will apply the medicine of generosity, love, patience, fellowship, endurance and kindness." If we act from that place as an act of will, then those angels are dominant in our lives and those angels will be dominant at death. And this brings us right face to face with a very profound principle…As we live, so shall we die. What you did in life will be expressed with incredible intensity at death. This is certain.

In the end, uplifting oneself is the fruit of wisdom and the desire for one's own benefit and the benefit of others.

This is the worldly dharma. This is the struggle we face everyday as we move through our incredibly complex society and try to be good people and we see injustice everywhere around us and we see good people suffering and evil people prospering. Know that nobody escapes and it's incumbent upon us and important to us to look to our own garden. This is the dynamic of the worldly dharma.

The holy dharma is the deep law of the creation. This is where we find the mystery of the movement of the life force inside the breath – the manifestation of the infinite awareness that we call mind, the infinite apparent creation. There are powerful mechanics involved. It is the ocean of the Great Light that sustains all, that is revealed with incredible force at the moment of death, at the Bardo Thodol, the interval between life and death when reality arises.

In fact you should understand that the deconstruction of one's being, the traversing of the Bardo, has one principle involved. It is designed to bring you into contact, bring you face to face with the Great Light, the Clear Light of Reality, in an ever-descending formula. In other words, it starts, "BANG! Here I am." You recognize the Clear Light of Reality at that moment; you're absorbed into it; the whole thing is over. Having lived a life of superstitious misunderstanding, you'll perhaps see the Great Light of Reality as a fearsome light of a billion suns that carries your certain destruction and what will you do? You will shun it in fear.

No matter how ferocious the mechanics of the Bardo Thodol are, they thrive on free choice. You have the choice to reject the Great Light. The price you pay is that you go down a step and the stakes of ignorance go up. From the very first moment of fearing the Great Light, you go down a step, the conditions become more complicated, and again the light presents itself. Again you have the opportunity to recognize the Clear Light as the light of God, as the light of consciousness. But you're not forced to recognize it. Again, if you reject it out of fear, you go down a step, the stakes go up, confusion intensifies, and once again, the Clear Light of Reality presents itself. Throughout the entire complexity of the interval between life and death, this is what's happening over and over again. You are brought face to face with the Clear Light of Reality – All you have to do is recognize it as such. You are absorbed into its nature and you become enlightened. It's simple.

No matter what, you could be the worst sinner; you could be Genghis Khan and have killed millions of people. At the moment of the dawning of the Great Light, if you recognize it as such, you absorb into the Great Light and you are enlightened. It's not vindictive. Genghis Khan killed a couple million people at least and realized "I need a really heavy-duty lama to save me." That was the reason the Dalai Lama was made the Dalai Lama. The 14th Dalai Lama, then just coming up in the hierarchy, was chosen. The word *Dalai* means great, or the greatest lama, and it was Genghis Khan who gave him that name. He was the great destroyer, so he needed the great savior. Anyway, that's just an aside.

The point is that the interval is the presentation of the Clear Light of Reality. You will emerge out of the fabric of your own life with all your conditioning.

It's an incredibly complex mathematical equation.

The balance of every thought, every emotion, every action weighing on your soul as a samskaric component, accumulates into a karma and that will define you individually. At the moment of the presentation of the Great Light you can say, "Life and death are the same. There is no difference between my identity and the quality of the Great Light." However, if you are confused and you have identified with the body, then the first fear is that the body is being destroyed. This throws the mind into turmoil and that turmoil generates panic, fear and a state of crisis, and we know that in that state of mind we tend to make less and less cogent decisions. This is one of the dramas of the moment of the death; it comes at you inexorably and even though you say, "Just give me a second to think, I need to just pull myself together", that will not be given.

Let me put it this way…The amount of time you have to pull yourself together will be the exact mathematical equation of your good and bad karma. If you presented a lot of good actions in your karma, then the Great Light will appear benign and approach softly. If you produced a lot of darker actions, the appearance of the Great Light will take on the characteristic of that darkness. In other words, it's a perfect mirror. It's consciousness.

In the cycle of life and death there are six states of consciousness through which we cycle. We have the Bardo of Life (1), which we understand primarily as the waking state. This is the envelope wherein life arises. We have the Bardo of the dream state (2). The dream state is the Bardo wherein the body consciousness falls away and we dream. We assemble and reassemble memory of mostly this life and past lives and we produce an entire world of the Bardo of the dream state. We have the Bardo of meditation (3), which is the experience of the fourth state – turiya.

We have the Bardo of the death process (4). This is the force of nature that's like being hit by enormous light and all of the components of mind-body-being are separated from each other. Then we have the Bardo of the after-death process (5). This is the interval where you are neither alive nor are you entirely inside the death process; there's a point in the middle where you're in transition. And then we have the Bardo of Rebirth (6).

This interval carries the entire Bardo Thodol. Inside this interval you will go through a series of confrontations with the Great Light, the Clear Light of Reality. In these confrontations there is one event after another where you are brought face to face with the Clear Light of Reality. This is where we see the principle of freedom of choice, free will at its most pure. At no point are you forced to choose one way or another. You are allowed to make your choice at every turn and then you inexorably experience the fruit of your choice. In the Bardo Thodol, the interval, this takes place instantaneously. In life when we have a desire sometimes it will seem like X amount of time will happen before the desire is fulfilled. It will always be fulfilled. It might not be fulfilled when you want it. It might occur in a different time. It might not be exactly in the same conditions, but having produced a desire, that desire will be fulfilled. Perhaps it will be fulfilled in death; life and death are the same. That's why they always say, be careful what you want. What you desire will always come to you.

Inside the Bardo Thodol you will go through a series of 100 confrontations with the Great Light. This number, 100, corresponds to the number of fibers that flow inside the three channels of ida, pingala and sushumna – left and right channel, central nerve and the brain, which is broken down into six quadrants. We know that the brain has six lobes. We also know that there are six chakras – one at the base of the spine, the region of the genitals, the navel, the heart, the throat, the forehead and the seventh chakra, the 1000 petaled lotus at the crown of the head. The chakra or the wheel at the base of the spine has four fibers; the wheel at the genitals has six fibers; the wheel at the navel has ten fibers; the wheel at the heart has twelve fibers; the wheel at the throat has sixteen fibers; the wheel at the forehead has two fibers. That's 50 fibers – 50 male manifesting on the right side, the pingala and 50 female shaktis manifesting on the left side, the ida. Going through the center of the two is the sushumna – the central nerve. This is the deep, abiding strand of consciousness. It is a fiber unto itself that absorbs the 100 fibers of relative and absolute reality.

The 50 fibers of male and female, which are on the left side of the body and the right side of the body, manifest in the Bardo as the Bardo demons and deities. Each one of them is the arising of the consciousness moving through each one of these fibers. All of these fibers – 4, 6, 10, 12 16, 2 – move throughout the subtle physical body. But they all end up in one place. The brain. These 50 on the left and these 50 on the right add up to 100 and they all go to different lobes of the brain. Now we also remember that the chakras at the base of the spine, at the genitals, at the heart, at the throat, have an elemental basis, which are the five elements of earth, water, fire, air and ether, and they are each associated with a color. Earth arises as yellow, water arises as green, fire arises as red, air arises as white and ether arises as blue. The earth is in the root chakra; water is in the second chakra, fire is in the third chakra, air is in the fourth chakra and ether is in the fifth chakra.

The Bardo deities are the 100 spontaneously arising forms of enlightenment. In their conditional reality they arise as demons or gods and goddesses. They're completely culture-centric. That's one of the reasons why I'm not tainting this talk with Tibetan terminology – because we're not Tibetans. For people that perhaps have a Judeo-Christian foundation, the deities will appear as angels and demons. They'll come up with something really great, don't worry. (Laughter) If you lived in India, they'd look like Shiva and Shakti and Ganesha and all that.

Question: Will they look like celebrities here?

Mark: The fact is, they do. There are celebrities that have become such a part of the group mind, they've entered the Bardo and they appear in your mind as Bardo deities. I'm not lying. (Laughter)

It's really funny. As an example, I've been preparing for this teaching all week. Bardo Thodol on the mind. Writing notes and meditating on it and just having to talk about it and last night I had this incredible Bardo dream where I was walking through the mandala of the Bardo Thodol, meeting the 100 deities, and the mandala looked like Burning Man and all of the sculptures were these incredible-looking deity gods and goddess looking beings – impossible to describe. All of these beings were coming out of the crowd and talking to me and some of them did actually look like movie stars. And they would be yellow or white or green or different colors and they would change colors and they would come up and present themselves to me and I would immediately recognize them as the deity that they were. You just know spontaneously. It's consciousness. Consciousness aligns with consciousness.

It's not like when you go in the Bardo that you have to remember the names of all those deities and what they look like. It's not going to be like that. Don't worry. What they do is they become an aggregate of all of your karmic conditionings – your good and bad karma, positive and negative thoughts and your expressions of the six poisons, which will manifest as demonic forms. Your expressions of the greater angels of love and generosity will manifest as benign forms. They will assemble out of the energies and essences of the elemental forces of earth, water, fire, wind, ether, the six chakras. Each of these fibers that are accumulated in the 50 fibers of the male Bardo deities and the 50 fibers of the female Bardo deities all assemble into the brain.

We know that the syllables of NAMAH SHIVAYA correspond to one of the five elements and the five lower chakras. The mantra OM NAMAH SHIVAYA then unifies the brain with OM as the unifying force. Then we have the six sections of the brain, each correlating with one of the chakras. The negative and positive karma suspends itself along each of these 50 fibers. If they are positive actions, positive samskaras, they look like little bright white mustard seeds. If they are dark negative actions, they look like little bits of tar. So as consciousness begins to disassemble, all of the qualities of the structure of identity start to fold into the three central nerves, ida, pingala and sushumna. As it manifests along the three central nerves, each of the six wheels with the four fibers at the base, six fibers at the loins, etc. all have these conditional karmas attached to them. It's like a circuit wire and the accumulated karma along each of these fibers exerts itself. So as it decentralizes, it sends this signal to the brain. You'll see that five universal families rule these 100 fibers. And these are the five basic lobes of the brain, plus the OM element, which is the gateway between the conditional reality and the universal reality.

What I'm stressing here is this is very, very mechanical. If you understand it as such, you'll be able to approach life with a much clearer picture of what it is that you're doing while you're living and what it is you're doing when it comes to the business of dying.

You should understand that the greatest opportunity you will have for enlightenment, the golden ticket, is handed to you at the moment of death. Get that through your skull. It's not something that should be feared. It is a golden opportunity.

Why? In life we are trapped in time because the entire apparatus of mind, body and the architecture of the assembly of being are assembled here, at *prthivi*, the firmness of the earth, which is very slow moving. That's why when we want something, it goes in here and it goes around, and maybe comes out here or maybe it comes out here. Chances are it doesn't ever come and it comes at the moment of death. And you go "Oh great, thanks, I was wondering when that was finally going to come to me." (Laughter) Just when you don't want it.

It's important to know that everything you want, you get. It's like the episode of the Twilight Zone where everything comes in with a twist; it has a hook. So here you are at the moment of death and you're trying to pull yourself together and leave under the Clear Light and then all your desires start coming in. "Oh, there's that and there's that." And you get distracted and you start thinking about your desires and you forget about the Clear Light. This is what everybody does. It sounds like a joke. Well, it is a joke and the joke is on you. (Laughter)

All of this information is stored in the 100 fibers. These 100 fibers are the structure and everything you think – conscious, subconscious or unconscious – appears there as a little byte of data. This is where you start to see again the first value of shaktipat. Shaktipat sends a throb of awakening down the central nerve in the crown of the head, down through the ida, pingala, sushumna – actually displaces and unwinds the samskaras of desire in all their formations, melts them away and clears them. This is a very dramatic example of the value of shaktipat. Getting shaktipat when you are aged 15, 20, 25 or 30 starts clearing all that stuff out. You'll notice that as you get shaktipat and go through your life, you'll experience less and less desire.

The first part of your life is ruled by desire. You want this and you want that and you judge the quality and happiness of your life by what you did get and what you didn't get. Shaktipat starts to clear all that stuff off. It's a giant throb of the Great Light that goes down the circuit of the central nerve, ida and pingala, and all of the six chakras – the 50 male and the 50 female fibers, the deities of the spontaneously arising Bardo – that grant enlightenment. When these fibers are clear, all they do is radiate enlightenment. That's their nature. They're of the nature of enlightenment, but they get encrusted by the samskaric and karmic conditions of your desire-nature. So when they start to fire up in the brain – the brain is just a computer; it's a receiver – if all of these bits and bytes of information that are on each of the fibers start striking the brain, the brain will just start chemically responding. At this moment of interval between life and death, all of the consciousness begins to absorb into the central nerve, ida and pingala, and fires up into the brain. The brain starts getting inundated; it's like a brainstorm.

As the onset of the Great Light is coming on, you think, "This is the end for me", and you have to deal with that moment of reckoning. And then the process of death begins and at the same time you start to deconstruct and all of these fibers begin to purge into the brain and the brain will just play everything out. And this is the dynamic of seeing every moment of your life. It really happens and it all happens with incredible detail. And that's the difference between life and death – the main difference. Life and death are the same, but the way the light operates is a little bit different.

In life we have a desire and it takes us forever to see the end of that desire. Even if we don't get it fulfilled, we'll carry that desire forever. In death, everything happens instantaneously. You will experience the cause of that desire; you will see the cause of that desire before you even had the desire; you will experience the fulfillment of that desire with incredible intensity. Just imagine, when you feel a desire granted in life, there's a kind of *rasa* that takes place, a kind of elixir takes place. The serotonin and dopamine run and there's a moment of pleasure, "Oh, I got my desire", and there's a little bit of happiness that goes through there. (Laughter) But when you look at it, there are only a few of those each day.

At the moment of death, every desire you ever had happens all at once and it becomes overwhelming.

This is the point of confusion. This is why they say that confusion arises at the moment of death because the brain is dumping its entire load all at once. At the same time there's the onset of the Great Light, and then the beginning dynamics of the fibers of the spontaneously arising enlightenment of the 100 deities, which are the 100 fibers of consciousness and they are all doing their thing. So it's a very dramatic moment of high tension, crisis, stress and confusion.

They basically say that if you wait until the moment of death to start figuring it out, you've waited too long. This is why with a person that has incarnated enough times, you'll tend to see that they will suddenly think, "Wait a minute, every time that happens to me, something bad happens. What I'm going to do is start meditating on the nature of existence very early in life. I'm going to seek out a Guru, somebody who has wisdom. I'm going to get shaktipat from them, which sends the impulse of awakening – it switches on all my stuff."

Because in a certain way what shaktipat does is trigger death and life simultaneously. In other words, what we unconsciously do is fold death away. One of the features of shaktipat is that it brings life and death together and so we begin to arise simultaneously in both realms. And so the clearing of the 100 fibers that takes place dramatically at death begins to happen, but it happens at a greater tempo. I know you've all experienced it; all of you have had shaktipat for a few years. Stuff just comes up. You feel it as a constant flow and it produces a kind of psychic pressure. At first it's very confusing. But after we become more seasoned, we learn to just let it go – like we're watching a movie. It comes up and it produces a pressure. When we first get shaktipat, we start getting attached to these spontaneously arising things and re-entangling ourselves. But after a while we get a little smarter about it. We don't attach. We stay detached. We just let it unfold and as it unfolds, it dissipates, it expiates, it is absorbed into the mind. The mind is absorbed into the Great Light and it just goes away. It's like pouring salt into water. It's like pouring water into water.

The fact is, with shaktipat you can get through the karmic detritus of this life and countless lives in one life, if you have the endurance and the strength to undergo that process. It will go faster and faster as you gain more capability, more skill.

If a person is only using the 100 fibers of consciousness and they're trapped in the worldly existence, going back and forth between manifesting jealousy and envy and anger, etc. and maybe there's a little bit of happiness and a little bit of generosity over here, but then it goes jealous again – that person will encumber themselves with this heavy light. When it releases, it's just like a rubber band under tension. You just twist, twist, twist and it kind of snaps. On the other hand, if it unfolds in the daily practice of meditation, the mindfulness of watching the quality of one's behavior, the quality of one's heart and mind, gives rise to love, gives rise to generosity. Generosity and love don't just happen. You'll never convince me that they do. You have to give rise to it as an act of will. Love is always present – generosity, patience and kindness. If you ever have the pleasure to meet a person that has generated that state where you feel complete absence of greed inside them, you feel the complete absence of jealousy. It's quite extraordinary. It's just not there. And what do you feel? You just feel a quality of luminosity. In most people you'll feel the different quality of poisons to a lesser or greater degree, but it's possible to dissipate and distill all of these qualities out of the system completely. That's like shedding 5,000 pounds of sheer karmic weight.

In the arena of life, this proposition is kind of an abstract. "Oh, that sounds interesting, maybe I'll do it, maybe I won't." And meanwhile you go on and do whatever you do in the privacy of your own room and that's fine, but at the moment of death, it matters. The exact weight of every ounce of envy, jealousy and greed will arise and it's not pleasant.

It's like a poison. What's amazing is that you can deny the presence of that poison in life, but you can't deny it in death. This is the day of reckoning that is present in life. The intention of every action is what is measured.

In the Bardo of Life we have positive and negative actions. In the Bardo of Dreams, we have the activity of the mind while the body is at rest, sleeping. In the Bardo of Meditation, we have the experience of meditation, concentration and discrimination – the refined behavior of mind – and we also have the force of one-pointedness – the cessation of thought and samadhi. The Bardo of Meditation should be understood as a doorway. We also have the Bardo of the Death process and the unfoldment of the elements, etc. And we have the Bardo of the After Death process. We also have the Bardo of the Rebirth process.

In all of these five Bardos, we are locked in – Bardo of Life, Bardo of Sleep, Bardo of Death, Bardo of After Death, Bardo of Rebirth. But in the Bardo of Meditation we can go to any of the other Bardos, which is why it is valuable as a basis of spiritual training. If you value your own well-being – just preparing for your own death, which is an absolute certainty, (only the moment of death is uncertain) – you will spend at least one hour out of your 24-

hour day meditating. Why? Because meditation strengthens the vitality of the five elements – earth, water, fire, air, ether. Meditation strengthens the vitality of the left and right channels. If we understand meditation very well, we can move our consciousness into the central nerve at will. That right there is the doorway into the Great Light. "Oh, here comes the Great Light, here comes all of my karma, Ahhhhh" – go into the central nerve, it's all over. You don't even have to fuss with it. But if you don't practice that everyday of your life up to the moment of death, you won't be able to pull it off. It's a moment of high performance. The dice are rolling and you can easily get entangled in your own karma. There's no rule that says you can't get entangled and you'll be lost in the dharma and you'll cycle again. But if you meditate everyday, and you keep yourself spiritually fit, in other words, your pranas are hot, all your chakras are blazing lights, your sushumna is open – you can get into the sushumna. You need to go into the sushumna everyday. Why? Because one day it's going to count. This is just the wisdom of practicing the holy dharma, understanding the mechanics of the creation.

Meditation is a doorway. From meditation you can travel from life to death without dropping the body. You can exist in the plane of life and plunge into the Great Light; you can exist simultaneously in the

Great Light and in the body. That's what samadhi is. And there are endless possibilities and potential.

You come to understand that awakening is inherent in all of these qualities of the creation as well as the formless void quality of the Great Light. When you understand the Great Light, you see that it is void. It has no quality; it pervades qualities. In other words, it pervades your mind. It is the luminosity of the mind. It pervades your body and the vitality of the life force within. What is life? What is the vitality that animates the senses? What is the vitality that animates the body? We see it take place in the mechanics of the pranas, etc.

We understand that the Bardo is a series of lights. The source of these lights is the mechanics of the five elements – the earth element as yellow, the water element as green, the fire element as red, the air element as white and the ether element as blue. The fibers, which come out of each of these seats, blend and operate and produce the mechanics of the appearance of the lights as each one of the 100 fibers is downloaded.

In the Bardo Thodol, the interval between life and death, you're completely deconstructed and each fiber, one at a time, deconstructs and produces the totality of itself. As it produces the totality of itself, it appears as that Bardo deity. And it will take place inside one of the five lobes of the brain and it will be a quality of 100 going into the five, like a mathematical equation.

The way we are structured is that the vitality of the life force has five pranas and they manifest as the descending energy, the ascending energy, the cyclical revolution energy, the expanding and contracting energy, and the infusing energy. The equation of life hangs inside these seats of the pranas in the body. It operates as a relationship between the three central nerves and the nine holes of the body. Going from bottom to up – the anus, the genital region, the navel, the mouth, the nostrils, the ears, the eyes, the forehead between the eyebrows and the crown of the head. These all act as stems off of the central nerve of the sushumna, ida and pingala, the 100 fibers and the six lobes of the brain. That is the Bardo Thodol.

Just imagine three calm rivers – ida, pingala and sushumna. Along those three rivers are the five chakras and their associated elements – earth, water, fire, air and ether and the sixth chakra which is OM, and is a void. Four fibers, six fibers, ten fibers, etc. – all going out through all the different parts of the physical and subtle physical and mental body, terminating in the brain. As we talked about in the Pratyahara Kunda, there is a quality of intention that flows from the seat of the navel, which is a kind of switching station between the lower body and the upper body. From here up is one deal; from here down is another deal. All of the 100 fibers going into the six lobes of the brain also have a terminus point, a flow of energy to each of the holes in the body.

As we meditate on the Bardo Thodol throughout this day, you'll feel that there is a very powerful descending energy that seems to be moving from above the head going down to the brain, down a little through the spinal column, striking each of the six wheels, animating each of the three rivers, illuminating the 100 fibers and reaching out and clearing the karma from the nine gates. The envelopes of the flesh, the bodily fluids, the breath, the complexion and the infusion are all interlocked.

So this is the basic description of the Bardo Thodol as it manifests on the side of life, on the side of death, and the interval in between.

In opening we described the architecture of the Bardo of Life and Death, the senses, organs and objects of the senses, the psychic states of the six poisons and the higher angels of love, generosity, kindness, etc., the structure of the mechanics of the Bardo Thodol as it appears in life with the three rivers, six chakras, six states of the Bardo of Life, Bardo of Dreams, Bardo of

Meditation, Bardo of Death (Chikhai), Bardo of After Death (Chonyid) and Bardo of Rebirth (Sidpa) – and the 100 fibers which are the 100 Bardo deities. The 100 fibers correlate to the fibers that flow from the six chakras, the six wheels that move up the three rivers – ida, pingala and sushumna, the six lobes of the brain and the elemental basis of the chakras that also permeate the fibers.

This is the structure of the holy dharma – the architecture of consciousness as it interacts with form. Consciousness and form arise simultaneously. One doesn't cause the other. They arise simultaneously. In this way you can more subtly understand what I mean when I say that life and death are the same. They're present simultaneously. It is attention that moves.

CHAPTER 2

THE PATHWAY OF THE TRANSITION

In this next stage we will see that the entire essence of the death process takes place with the breath and the expression of the Bodhicitta. It is its absolute foundation. How do we begin every single meditation? We begin the cycling of the breath, the vibration of the SoHam, and attentiveness to the space between the breaths. This is the presence of the empty void nature of the Clear Light. We raise Bodhicitta. It is the enlightenment factor of mind. It would be appropriate to say that every time you sit down to meditate and begin this process, you are practicing for the moment when it most counts. Having done it 100,000 times in life, it becomes easy to do at the moment of death. It's the essential move. The ability to do this is the key to auspicious unfoldment in the intermediate state between life and death.

If you learn to arouse the Bodhicitta, generate the

SoHam and concentrate on the space between the breaths, there is a great strengthening of the presence of being, of consciousness, of spiritual forces if you learn to assemble the life force, the Kundalini and the mind. Then as you are enduring the traumatic moment of the separation of our mind from our body, you have the presence of mind to hold yourselves together within the SoHam and with the arousal of the Bodhicitta.

It is the Bodhicitta that makes possible the recognition of the Great Clear Light at the moment it arises. At the beginning of every meditation, you sit down, you cycle the breath, you arouse Bodhicitta. What are you doing? You are paying obeisance to the Clear Light within, touching it while you are alive. In this way we again have a very powerful example of the similarity between life and death – in this case you are touching the Great Light while still in possession of the body.

One of the ideas of spiritual training, of a daily meditation practice, is familiarity with contacting the Great Light. When you touch it within yourself at the seat of the Boddhicitta in the center of the body, it is the Great Light that you touch. Feel it, come to know it, absorb into it and make it your friend so that in the throes of the death process, you will recognize it when it appears.

The fibers of your ida and pingala, the left and right channels, will be very strong and sound; they will be open from the base of the spine to the crown of the head. All of the six wheels will be open and brilliantly vibrating, conducting that light into the brain. The 100 fibers – the 50 male Bardo deities and the 50 female Bardo deities will be purified – having been saturated throughout one's life by the vibration of the Great Light and the holy dharma of the manifestation of the Bardo Thodol in life. The karma will have been studiously, patiently and thoroughly dissolved while living, so we will not be encumbered at that dramatic moment of death. The skandas, the piles of karmas generated by each of the senses, will be diminished and eliminated and the pathways of the nine gates will be clear and open.

We will understand the map of our internal spiritual world as clearly as the back of our hand. This will be very helpful in the process of understanding what is happening, as it is happening. We will not be thrown into a reactive state of crisis. We will recognize the onset of the symptoms of death and we will gather ourselves together and prepare for the great leap. And while it is true that all living things tremble before death, we will have the presence of mind to pull ourselves together, arouse our courage, and prepare for this most profound and significant of all journeys. Again, I say, the moment of death is a golden opportunity for enlightenment. Ninety-nine people out of one hundred who generate enlightenment do so at the moment of death.

It's when you become very versed in the idea that life and death are the same, that the potential of the samadhi condition – which is the absorption of one's identity, the absorption of one's mind into the Great Light – while still in possession of the body, can occur. Why wait?

It is also true that, as is often said in the scriptures by the wise, profound meditation is a replication of the death process. This is the origin of fear that meditators run into when meditation becomes very strong. Their meditation gets stronger and stronger and stronger and there's a point where the absorption of identity, the absorption of mind into the Great Light, begins to occur. People mistake this event for death and withdraw, pull back from their practice, or enter into an unstable psychic state. What the Bardo Thodol expresses is the inevitability of the moment of death, its certainty and the wise preparation for that moment.

THE THREE STAGES

The process of the movement through the Bardos is the same for everyone. All sentient beings in this world system unfold through the Bardos regardless of belief, religion or culture. Obviously these different cultural factors will produce a different content of karmic conditioning along the pathway to the 100 fibers and this will affect the appearance of the dream. But the underlying process is the same.

The Bardo is broken up into three events. Each of these stages of Bardo has a title. The first one is called the *Chikhai Bardo*. This is the arousal of the symptoms of death and the appearance of the Great Light.

The *Chonyid Bardo* is the Bardo where having come face to face with the Clear Light, one has run in fear from it and taken refuge in the karmic conditions of the false refuge of individual identity. The Chonyid Bardo is thus the Bardo wherein the karmic conditions begin to play out inside a psychic dream as each of the contents of the 100 fibers brings you face to face with the Clear Light in an ever progressing condition, step by step, through the 100 deities.

The Chonyid Bardo is the step-by-step manifestation of the 100 deities and their karmic content, and is brought about by having confused the appearance of the Great Light as something fearsome and taken the false refuge of individual identity. One plunges into the Bardo and thus has to face each of the Bardo deities, which are broken up into two categories: The peaceful deities and the wrathful deities. There are 42 peaceful deities, the quiescent elements that tend to be of the deep underlying fabric of psyche and of the nature of the higher angels. And there are 58 wrathful deities, which take place in the architecture of the mind-structure. They are characterized as the brain mass, the underlying (what we call euphemistically) lizard brain, and the primordial brain. Thus they will appear in sets of ever increasingly wrathful and terrifying images. No matter how wrathful or terrifying, all that is ever happening is that you are being brought face to face with Clear Light in the form of your own thought-constructs. Nothing outside of you or alien to you is contacting you in any way. It is the substance of your own mind essence, arising directly as the Clear Light, the Great Light of Reality, in the form of the 100 spontaneously enlightened Bardo deities – 42 peaceful, 58 wrathful. This is the Chonyid Bardo.

The third Bardo is called the *Sidpa Bardo*. This is the Bardo of having gone through the entire cycle of the 100 fibers, the 100 spontaneously enlightened deities and having taken the false refuge of belief in the reality of the thought-constructs that are expressed in each of the fibers. One has essentially stayed attached to the form of individual being, refusing to recognize the import of the Clear Light and its nature as truth, seeing it as Jung would say, "the other, the shadow." It is rejected and we take the false refuge of individual identity. "I want to exist separately from the Great Light" and it's a free choice. You have that choice. And having made that choice 100 times through the Chonyid, you then enter the Sidpa Bardo.

Sidpa Bardo is the Bardo wherein you select the rebirth of your new body, which world it will be in, what form will you be. Will you be plant, animal, fish, human, Preta, God or Goddess? Again, at any one point in the Sidpa one can select to merge with the Great Light and as an act of will, close the womb gate.

In the case of enlightened birth, a Bodhisattva or a being of an enlightened personality will also use the Sidpa Bardo as a mode of entry, but their choices of entry are, of course, much wider and they will select birth for the highest reason of service, of doctrine, of power, of compassion, of love, of action. I've had the opportunity to meet all kinds.

So with this basic architecture of the three forms of Bardo: Chikhai, Chonyid and Sidpa, let's look at the reflexes inside these movements.

First off, the Bardo lasts anywhere from a microsecond to 49 days. It is a microsecond for a person who, when the Clear Light appears, immediately recognizes it as such, and is absorbed into Clear Light. The event is complete. They can choose to stay in the Clear Light as an enlightened being – incarnate, completely absorbed, and from this place reincarnate at will. For a person who chooses to reincarnate, or for a person who does not recognize the Clear Light, the actual period of time from the moment of death through the Chikhai Bardo, through the Chonyid Bardo, through the Sidpa Bardo, is 49 days.

Human incarnation is considered to be a final form, a complete form, which is to say that once you have incarnated as a human being, you will not fall below the complexity of that form and you will continue to incarnate in the human realm until enlightenment. The cycle of the movement from the moment of death to rebirth in the basic human being that is dealing with all the complexities of the Bardo, with minimum amount of training, having to undergo the entire process, is 49 days. Most of you have incarnated thousands of times and you have never been off the earth plane for more than 49 days at a time, which explains why you are so tired all the time. Not only is the Bardo totally murder, but then you have to be reborn.

Question: I thought you said there was a 60-day vacation?

Mark: Anything can happen. Anything is possible. Everything is about connections. If you have connections with the enlightened sangha, with beings in higher planes or with deities in higher planes that can take your case under consideration, then you can get a better deal. So the Bardo is a complete replication of every principle we know here on earth. It's very familiar in that way.

At that moment the best connection to have is a Guru that is supported by a lineage. You cannot get a better connection. In that situation you can get an outcome well beyond your own abilities. The services of the Guru and lineage actually come in and give you shelter and improve your condition beyond measure.

At the appearance of the symptoms of death you'll begin to feel a dissipation of the life vitality. The vitality of the life force will tend to withdraw into the core. It will move out of the extremities – the body kind of rolls up like a toothpaste tube – coldness in the hands and the feet, up the legs, into the core, bodily heat begins to dissipate; loss of consciousness and the appearance of the next world in the psychic frame begins to appear in dreams.

It is better to have a life wherein death can approach by degrees. It will come and there's an aura that causes all of these events: the absorption of the heat into the core; the movement of the vitality, the prana, out of the extremities; the dimming of the light of the mind; and the falling away of the complexion of the body. This word 'complexion' would be the infusion of the body where the life force and the body are starting to separate. Anybody who has had the honor of watching a human being die is very familiar with all of these stages.

If your understanding, your connection to the worldly dharma and the holy dharma is strong, it is best to meet death on the terms of meditation. Enter into the meditation Bardo, wherein you are in the widest sweep of potentials. You are sitting up, your spine is vertical to the earth and because of the magnetic field of the earth, there is a natural movement of verticality to the movement of the life force inside the body that is relative to the spine in the physical body and relative to the ida, pingala and sushumna in the subtle physical body. Of course the mechanics of the mind are in the 100 fibers that are concentrated at the heart and in the brain.

You will find there is much less confusion if you are sitting up. What will happen is that as the symptoms of death appear, there will be the stages of the withdrawal from the extremities into the core, the pranas will withdraw into the core, the psychic heat will withdraw into the core, the infusion, the complexion of the body, will begin to separate and you'll feel all of a sudden like your body is letting you go. This is the moment of recognition that you are in the moment of death. What will happen is that the breath will become slower and slower. You will fall off of the table of the waking state and you'll exist only in the psychic state. Your breath will be very faint and the breath will move out of the physicality and will only move in the central nerve and in the seat of the Bodhicitta. You'll find yourself breathing only in the three rivers.

This is where you see very dramatically that life and death are attenuated to the breath. When the breath moves, the mind moves. When the mind moves, the life force, the vitality, moves. So in the in-breath, the vitality is moving and in the out-breath, the vitality is moving. In the space in between the breaths, the vitality is void and empty. Our life is like a florescent bulb. You know that a florescent bulb switches on and off so fast, it seems like a steady light. But the poles of the light are a positive in-breath and out-breath. The space in between the breaths is the place of the appearance of the Great Light. It is the void center. It is empty. As the breath dwindles, it will dwindle and stop. In other words, having tick tock tick tock, your consciousness principle will stop in the space between the breaths. This is the moment of death. This is the moment of void arising and the Clear Light will arise with incredible force, right then, right there.

The prana will withdraw into the left and right channels and begin to fly down the ladder of the three rivers. In the moment as the Bardo of Life falls away, the oceanic presence of the Great Light of ten billion suns will arise. This is the arising of death.

Now there is an interesting variant here. This is where the difference is in a person that is spiritually prepared and trained, and has made their systems sound. Their nervous system, their subtle physical body, their mental body, will quite literally conduct the force of the Great Light. It is possible and it is known that very advanced yogis, Siddhas, sages and beings of very advanced consciousness have the ability to sit in this state virtually as long as they want. It is typical of advanced yogis that they will go into that state of consciousness anywhere from 3-7 days. Their body will become very, very still. Their body will be upright and they will be merged with the Great Light. There are some cases where advanced yogis will merge with the Great Light and have their bodies buried and they will exist in eternity, present inside the body, merged with the Great Light. This is a dynamic action of power and compassion, committing the death state of their incarnation to be a presence of the Clear Light inside the appearance of the world.

If you are a being of yogic capability, the easiest way to stabilize the appearance of the Clear Light as it arises is – as the breath stops and the life force begins to fly down the three rivers – to give rise to the Bodhicitta. By arousing Bodhicitta, you become aware of a white bindu at the crown of the head. This is a practice that we've done in this Center.

The White Bodhicitta is the atmospheric essence of the Great Light inside the body. By yogically capturing it in a state of deep samadhi, profound meditation, you can cause the White Bodhicitta to sink into the region of the heart. The White Bodhicitta is the essence of the right side, the pingala. The White Bodhicitta is the yang principle.

At the seat of the navel, is the seat of the Red Bodhicitta. It will appear as a small bindu. A bindu is like a small seed. If you cause that to rise from the navel to the heart and have the white and the red meet at the heart (then you feel) "the two essences of the Great Light are the remnants of my body – they are the Clear Light." Because you will no longer be in the body when you do this, you are saying, "I am now the White Bodhicitta and I am now the Red Bodhicitta." And you can exist in this state as long as you want. It is typical of high lamas, advanced Gurus and advanced yogis, to stay in this state of consciousness anywhere from 3-7 days. The last Karmapa stayed in a state of absolute absorption into the Clear Light for 40 days.

When you're dealing with the burial of such a being, they say that you let the body sit in state for up to 40 days. There's a subtle remnant of karma that they're dealing with, oftentimes because they've taken on so much karma in their spiritual work, they sit inside the intermediate state to catch up on all the work that was left at the end of that life. And you will see that it will go anywhere from three to seven, up to forty days. I've heard of several years. We went to see the Temple of Jnaneshwar. He went into the samadhi I'm describing somewhere in the 12th century and he's there now to this day. When you go there, you can feel him.

If you are dealing with the tending of a body of this kind, there's a great notation: "Wait until a yellow fluid begins to flow out of all of the orifices of the body and then that is the signal that the karmic work that the soul is doing is done and now you can either cremate him or bury him or whatever you're going to do."

If we're dealing with a person of basic abilities, an average human being, we see that the onset of the symptoms of death are the same – the withdrawal of the life force from the extremities, withdrawal of the heat into the core, loss of the complexion, all the agility of the body will go away, the dimming of the senses and the mind will seem to go distant. You can be sitting right next to them and you can still talk to them, but you can feel them reaching through folds as if they're fading away, as if they're being covered. With such a person, it's not so necessary that they be sitting up. What is best at that point is to roll the body over on its right side – put the right side of the body down, left side of the body up – you'll see the pulsing in the arteries in the final stages of life. It's also possible that by pressing the sleep nerve in the throat (the carotid artery of the left and right side of the throat, pressed simultaneously) you can move them into the sleep state, and at that point they will fade away and meet death. You'll see the breath fade and at one point between the in-breath and the out-breath, the breath will stop. This is the moment of death. At this moment the person is experiencing the onset of the Great Light. It's right away.

Question: Did you say wait before rolling the person over on to the right side?

Mark: As the symptoms of death are approaching. In this scenario I'm talking about a regular person. A friend or relative, who has not undergone spiritual training, will be more relaxed lying down, but it's better to roll them on their right side. That way their spine is not perpendicular to the earth and they have their right side down. The right side is the side of the body in the world. The left side is the spiritual world and the mental world. If you turn them onto the right side, their central nerve is open. If they're lying flat on their back, there's a compromise by the gravitational pull of the earth and it just makes it more difficult for them. At that moment they are experiencing the Great Light. The energy basically flies down the central nerve and the ida and pingala. It's one of the reasons why you want to press the artery on the neck and the sleep nerve that will cause their mind to calm down. Now with a regular person, the appearance of the Great Light will usually last only a second or two. All of a sudden they will experience the manifestation of ten billion suns in their consciousness and they will either enter it or they will withdraw from it. If they enter it, then they realize the Clear Light as empty, as void, as the nature of the truth, and the Bardo is completed, the Bardo is fulfilled. It must be understood that it is not to be feared. It is the Great Light. It is the truth. It is God.

At this time the prana is in the central nerve. A person of normal ability and training, with X amount of religious training, will usually have as an ideal some form of the Great Light, a form of the Godhead or Goddess that they've become attached to, for instance, Meher Baba, or for a Christian – Jesus Christ, for a Muslim – Allah, for a Jew – Yahweh. If there has been minimal yogic training, but there has been religious training and the belief in a form of God has been adopted, the person in their last moments should think of that form of God and they should know that when the Great Light arises, that is the true light of God. This of course makes it easier to accept. "Oh, if the Great Light is my God, I won't be afraid."

If a person is a being of spiritual training, they should be sitting up. They should be prepared for the onset of the Great Light, meditate on their Guru. As the Great Light emerges, flies down the left and right channel and the central nerve, you catch it in the Bodhicitta. It's a very cool maneuver because then at that moment you achieve enlightenment. If you can hold the White Bodhicitta and the Red Bodhicitta for even a single second at the seat of the heart, you will receive complete enlightenment. It will not feel different or foreign because having raised Bodhicitta 100,000 times in life, it will be the same. The person will stay absorbed in this state for at least three days; or if the person is yogically trained, seven days. If conditions permit, the body should be allowed to lie in state, untouched. As they go into the Great Light, there will be a process of equilibrium as the soul merges in the Great Light and all that manifestation is completed.

In a spiritually trained person, there is incredible potential at this time to advance one's incarnation. If one desires to incarnate in the enlightened lineage, it is possible to give rise to signifiers within the mind that will select the future incarnations of enlightened births. This is the pathway of the enlightened sangha, the great Gurus. The Clear Light expiates all karma.

At this point the being, the traveler, exists as a form of thought, a kind of thought body. And they will be undergoing ecstatic transformation into a being of light. At the end of any given amount of time – they say anywhere from the snap of the fingers, to the length it takes to eat a meal, to three days, seven days, to infinity in rare cases – if a person has entered the Clear Light, as the karma is burned off you will see a yellow fluid begin to flow from the orifices of the body. Then the complete exit of the body has taken place. There will be some form of sign at the crown of the head – a spot of blood or a swelling.

As the darshan with Clear Light ends, there is a secondary event as the traveler comes out of absorption and goes into the next condition. The Clear Light first arises as the light of ten billion suns; after that it goes void – you are not there, you're not aware that you're doing anything. You've absorbed and the karma between the three conditioned bodies and the fourth physical body is all being taken care of. Now this is all relative. Anything can happen. If the body is disturbed or if there is only a partial acceptance of the Great Light, etc., that will affect things. Everything is high performance and everything counts.

You have to understand that there is complete integration between life and death. It's all present now. The movement of the Bardo is not some magical world. It's like this world. Dream after dream.

As this first phase of the darshan of the Great Light completes, there is a secondary appearance of the Clear Light, although it is said to be lesser. Now if a person has successfully absorbed, then the whole thing is over. Everything has been complete and is done. If a person of middling ability did not understand that the Great Light occurred and withdrew in fear from the Great Light (the Great Light will not overwhelm you) – you'll go "OK, fine" and at that point you are making a selection for the apparition of Bardo. At this point the Chikhai Bardo is complete and you are ready to go into the Chonyid Bardo and the karmic apparitions appear.

The Chonyid Bardo assembles itself along the

five elements – yellow, earth; green, water; red, fire; white, air; blue, ether. Each of these Bardos are infinite universes and produce thousands of countless dreams cast in the color of that element as it dissolves.

If we've already absorbed into the Clear Light during Chikhai, then the Great Light has fired and poured down the three nerves, ida, pingala and sushumna. What is present in the center of the ida, pingala and sushumna? – the six chakras and the five elements. If we've absorbed into the Great Light, all of that is processed in the Great Light – "whoooo" and it's gone, it's out. Or one can stay inside the body for eternity and exist through eternity.

That's the case with Bhagawan Nityananda. When we go to Ganeshpuri, one of the reasons that place is so powerful is that Bhagawan is still there inside his body, underneath that statue. It's not like it's radiating from the bones – his enlightenment was so profound that he can exist in eternity as well as the last placement of that body. When you are in that temple, you know yourself to be in the presence of Nityananda. Nityananda was never human – we've spoken about this – he's an emanation from the yogic paradises, a sage level mentality, which is to say his existence, his mind, is infinite.

So the Chikhai Bardo is the place where we've gone through the advent of the Great Light. Let's say that the person reacted in fear to the ten billion suns but then the mind repulsed and took false refuge in the identity of the individual, hoping to hold on to the body. Now even so, when the person has had the darshan of the Great Light for one second, they're kind of switched off; the blow of the Great Light just kind of switches them off but they haven't absorbed. They'll tend to be inside the body for two or three days. That's why it's best not to touch the body for two or three days. During that time they will be conscious of everything going on in the creation, everything going on in the room. If you are a friend or a loved one sitting next to a person that is dying, they will be aware of your presence in the room. You can talk to them. They will be going through a kind of disorientation, thinking that they are still alive and they will be in a dream state and they will somehow incorporate what you are doing and what you're going through into a dream. At the same time, they will begin to slide between the worlds. They'll begin to see their old life passing through their mind. The Chikhai Bardo is very, very stable. The onset of the karma hasn't occurred yet and so the Bardo is revealed for what it is, an endless dream.

It is very interesting. They will be seeing all the people in their lives internally. They will begin sliding between the planes of their next reality. If it is good karma, they will be seeing the higher planes and scenes of happiness. If it is bad karma, they'll be seeing terrifying scenes of hell. This is the beginning of that whole process. At the end of three days, they will come out of it, so to speak, and the Great Light will appear again, of lesser quality. Again at this moment, having gone through those three days of dreams, it's possible for them to say, "Now I remember, this is the Great Light of truth." And they can merge. And again, it's over.

This is a very interesting aside, that while you are in that three day dream, you will be able to see your body lying in the bed, you will try to re-enter it and you won't be able to. The gate of death has closed and you cannot re-enter the body although you'll be able to see it. You'll see people around you mourning, you'll see your wake, you'll see people dividing up your worldly goods, you'll know the true heart of everybody in the room exactly without the slightest prevarication, because it's the Clear Light. You still have all the reactions. "Why is everybody so unhappy." "Hey, where do you think you're going with my stuff?" It's kind of funny. And you'll see your body and you'll try to re-enter it.

What's interesting is when you look down at your body you won't see your body with your face.

This is where the medicine wheel arises. If you understand the concept of the medicine wheel, we are an aggregate assembly of a 12-house zodiac that is personified by animals and combinations of planetary forces. We have the year of the tiger, the year of the dragon, the year of the horse, etc., and they're all parts of the structure of the medicine wheel. So if you were born in the year of the horse, your Bardo dream will take on the appearance of a horse. When you look down at your body, you won't see your body but you'll see a dead horse. If you were born in the year of the tiger, you won't see your body but you'll see a dead or dying tiger, etc.

Question: That's if you're indoctrinated into that way of thinking, right?

Mark: The medicine wheel is nature so it will select a form. Whatever it is that you are the exact chemistry of – your mental condition, the year of your astrological birth, the astrological position of the planets, etc., there will be a correlating animal. It is the force of nature. It is the medicine wheel. One thing that will happen over the course of your life is your animal will appear in your dreams. You form a good relationship with it, (getting into sorcery) and it will be an ally; it will give you really good information, as you need it. It's a way of communicating with the spirit world.

As all of this completes, it's the end of the Chikhai Bardo and the Great Light appears for the second time, in a lesser force but just as complete. Often times this is the place where people join the Great Light because they've played out the karma and the panic has subsided and they can merge with the Great Light. So it's very fair.

Now this becomes the beginning of the Chonyid Bardo because the energy has completely animated the spinal cord. The spinal cord is connected to the ida, pingala and sushumna; ida, pingala and sushumna are connected to the six chakras, the six chakras are connected to the 100 fibers, the six chakras are the basis of the five elements and the five elements are connected to the nine gates. This is where the karmic conditioning of the 100 fibers begins. And the first beginning process of this is the collapse of the elements. They will start with the earth element and the elements basically dissolve one into the other. In other words, they roll up like a tube of toothpaste. (See diagram.)

The earth element is at the base of the spine and it is yellow in color and it is the nature of earth, so one experiences violent earthquake rumblings and thunder, shaking and all loss of physical strength.

As earth absorbs into the water, one sees images of water, floods and the symptoms of death begins with the drying up of the fluids.

As the water collapses into fire, intense burning and dream of fire happens. The dreams will all be of a red cast, a red color. In the symptoms of death, it first manifests as the diminishing of the inner heat into the core.

As fire dissolves into air, vast wild wind occurs and the mind begins to fade.

As air dissolves into ether, all sensory perceptions switch off. You lose contact with the world in the symptoms of the death phase and this is the advent of the Clear Light.

At the end of the dissipation and collapse of the senses, again the Clear Light arises. It's possible to recognize it as such, withdraw from any attachment to the false refuge of separate mind and body and merge into the Clear Light.

THE PHOWA

What I want to discuss before we go to the next stage of the Chonyid Bardo is the relationship of liberation through the power of the *phowa*. This is the value of the relationship to the Guru. Phowa means transference of consciousness. This is actually the money shot. The relationship with the Guru is the relationship with the Great Light. Thus it is important to find the Guru that has had a Guru; that that Guru has had a Guru; that that Guru has had a Guru and thus you have contact with a spiritual force that is called a lineage that goes from the present into the endless mists of time, all arising with the incredible spiritual force of the Great Light, incarnate.

If you have met a Guru in the physical form, you should know that the Great Light is present in that person. What they have essentially done is they've gone through the Bardo process and held on to the body. In other words, they've gone into the Great Light, dissolved into the Great Light, and through some wild way, managed to hold onto the body. The body of the Guru is the place where the Great Light is moving through a physical frame. The dynamic advantage of having a relationship with a Guru is forming a relationship with a being that is running the Great Light through their physical mind, through their body, through their heart, and through their spirit, while being physically incarnate.

In our case, what we do every day when we meet during our events is I show you the pathway of the transference of consciousness – how to move consciousness from the Bardo of the waking state, into the dream state, into the state of meditation, into the state of samadhi, through the state of death and all the way to the Clear Light and back. That's what a profound meditation is.

Nirvikalpa is a complete cycle of the Bardo. When you're sitting with a teacher that is in Nirvikalpa, he is showing you – expressing without words but through actual example – the path of the Bardo Thodol. He shows you what it feels like as the individual identity melts away, as the Great Light appears and fires down the sushumna, ida and pingala, as each of the elements are absorbed, as all of the chakras catch the light of the Great Light, fire up into the brain, and the brain is transformed into the vibration of the Great Light, which is what happens at the moment of recognition of the Great Light in the first Chikhai Bardo.

For everybody in this room, what I'm about to tell you is the whole thing. Because you're connected to a Guru, you have three ways to become enlightened. One – receive shaktipat and awaken, which in essence means that you go through the entire Bardo Thodol and hold on to the body. Two – realize the Great Light at death. Three – if you have not managed to do that by the time the moment of death arises, there is an opportunity to practice the phowa, the transference of consciousness.

Because of your relationship with the Guru and the connection of that teacher to the lineage, you have been living with an incarnation of the Great Light. This stable expression of the Great Light has a personality and so there is a quality of ease. One of the things you're supposed to be doing while we stay together is just watch what it looks like. It's not something that you see everyday and it's something that bears examination. This is your future. It will either happen to you while you hang onto the body or it will happen to you at the moment of death.

The process of the phowa is simple. At the moment of the Great Light, you grab the ida and pingala and absorb into them and bring the absorption into the manifestation at the seat of the Bodhicitta. If you have contact with a living Guru, by all means the Guru should be made aware of the fact that you are dying. The Guru will come to that place of death and be present in the room while you go through the process. It will be just like a meditation. You will feel the presence of the Nirvikalpa that is present in the Guru, present in the room. The Guru will both be in the body and in the Great Light simultaneously and thus you will have a stable connection to the moment of transference. Not only that but you have a quality of relaxation too because there's a familiarity. If you happen to be on another side of the planet and the event of death strikes you and it's not possible to generate physical contact with the Guru, you should generate the prayer of calling the Guru from afar and the Guru will come to you in the inner planes.

Essentially the Guru will aid you in the phowa, which is the manifestation of the stabilization of the Bodhicitta – the balancing of the White Bodhicitta and the Red Bodhicitta at the seat of the heart. As we've all practiced the Bodhicitta together – we do it at retreats and Intensives – what you notice is that the Great Light of the Bodhicitta flows down the ida and pingala and floods them with the Great Light, flows up into the brain and floods it with the Great Light, strikes each of the chakras and floods all of the 100 fibers with the Great Light and floods up into the brain. There is a quality of meditation at this point by stabilizing the person inside the body, inside the Great Light.

If the person is highly trained, he or she is capable of shutting off the eight gates. There are eight lower gates in terms of the process of exiting the body. You exit the body out of one of the holes of the body. The lower gates are the genitals and the anus. These are the worst gates to exit from. Then there is the navel and the gates of the holes in the head – two ears (counted as one exit), two nostrils (counted as one exit), two eyes (counted as one exit), the mouth and the forehead between the eyebrows. The phowa is the ability to block the eight lower gates. It's an expression of will. The consciousness is absorbed out of the external energies of the 72,000 fibers and merged into the ida and pingala, merges into the sushumna. The sushumna merges into the Bodhicitta at the seat of the heart. All of the gates of the holes in the head, the navel, the genitals and anus are blocked by the intent. It's impossible for the spirit to exit, so the spirit travels up the sushumna and exits out the crown of the head. That moment merges into the Dharmakaya; it merges into the Great Light.

It's important to remember that the seat of the Guru is at the crown of the head. There is a triangular patch under the skull in the brain. One of the reasons why they say that the grace of the Guru is necessary to generate the transmission of the Great Light into the body, the Shaktipat, is that the Great Light is throughout and pervading the whole, but the ability to draw it down the central nerve requires intense yogic skill – the ability to stop the mind and draw the Great Light into the central nerve. This is what I mean by saying, "by having practiced yoga." If you do the pratyahara everyday you can merge the Great Light into the central nerve at will. That way when it comes to the moment of death, when it counts, you can do that. There's a performance factor here if you are yogically trained, holding the Great Light in a state of equilibrium at the seat of the Bodhicitta for as long as possible. It's a quality of performance; it's a quality of an expression of enlightenment. It's a kind of vitality, a kind of dance there. You're overpowering death.

As the eight lower gates are blocked, everything is absorbed and gathered at the seat of the heart, flies up into the brain and flies out through the crown of the head like a bird flying out of a skylight. And you are enlightened.

The seat of infusion is right there at the crown of the head. The seat of the Guru is at the crown of the head, under the cap of the skull, the Brahmarandra, the soft spot at the brain when we are first born, the point where the infusion of life takes place in a human being. The point of infusion produces an atmosphere because the Great Light sits in the crown at the sahasrar and that is infinite light and outside of time. Below that is inside of time, conditional reality – the physical body, subtle physical body and mental body are conditioned and subject to time – in other words, transitory. At the point of the Brahmarandra, the seat of the Great Light and the White Bodhicitta, it's infinite and unchanging. It is the Dharmakaya, the Dharmadhatu, the ocean of consciousness.

Spiritual teaching is always encoded. They say bring the Guru to the crown of your head. One becomes a Guru because he's had an infusion. He's taken out all of his individual identity and now that's replaced with Great Light. Not only are you meeting the one Guru, but also you are meeting that Guru's Guru and that Guru's Guru and that Guru's Guru. All are present in the one. So it's a very stable presence, a very stable force. It's of the nature of the Great Light and it's of the nature of liberation.

At this moment of death when the Great Light dawns, you stabilize the Bodhicitta inside your system, you pray to the Guru and bring the Guru to the crown of your head. The seat of the Guru is actually a piece of the brain mass. If a person has received grace from a Guru, in other words, they are taken on by that Guru, then that piece of that brain mass is active and that piece of brain mass is of the nature of the Great Light. It's already present and so all you have to do is bring the Guru to the crown of the head. Because that brain mass has become very, very active, the light travels up the crown of the head and you just fly up, fire through it. It's a triangular shape and it represents the three worlds, the point where the body, speech and mind are divided. The one is divided into the three. Just like the OM. (See Diagram.) The crescent and the dot – the crescent is the infinite creation; the dot is the infinite ocean of the Clear Light; the triangle is just right there so your consciousness principle is merged into the central corridor, the central nerve. All of the eight other gates are blocked. (See diagram.)

The Guru comes to the crown of the head and an

irresistible force of infinite attraction draws your consciousness principle up the sushumna to the seat at the crown of the head. You blast through the Brahmarandra, you merge into the Great Light – You're enlightened! That's very easy to do if you have a Guru because that's all the Guru is hanging around waiting to do for you. As soon as you're ready, that's it. (Laughter) I mean we can do it now, we can do it later, it's up to you because it's always up to you. That's what it comes down to.

In the Bardo of Life we have all these distractions and we all love the Guru and we want to merge with the Great Light but we have all these other things going on and just having all these other things going is enough to hold you here. You had some desires when you were ten years old and you had some more desires when you were eighteen and on and on and now the whole thing is a disaster, but you still have those desires on the books because those desires produce a karmic connection and they have to play out in time. If you're able to let go of all of that at anytime, what I'm describing will occur. And you can even keep the body. Everybody really wants to keep the body and if you really want to keep the body, this is the way to do it. Go into Samadhi now.

What's great about the moment of death is the temporal quality of time loses its hold. The body is gone. You still have the karmic impressions but it's possible to override them because they're loosening their hold. There's a moment where everything has loosened its grip. This is where you practice phowa. Phowa is what you will all do at the moment of death. When you feel like you're dying, you'll pull yourself together, get all your affairs in order, you'll go through the stages of the loss of physical strength, the loss of vitality in the extremities, the loss of heat to the core, the loss of motor skills, the loss of vitality, the dimming of the senses and the dimming of the mind. "This is it; I'm going." Get to your place of power wherever it is, your meditation pad most likely, and you pull yourself together, and as the quality of the breath starts to slow and deepen, you'll feel the breath fall off the physical body. The physical body will stop breathing. You'll know yourself to be breathing only in sushumna. At that moment the body has died and you're still inside the body. That's the moment at the advance of the Great Light to produce the phowa. Block off the eight gates and bring the Guru to the crown of the head. The appearance of the Great Light and the movement of the grace of the Guru drawing to the crown of the head will happen simultaneously – or you can choose to hold in for three or four or seven days or seven centuries.

Most of you as a first incarnation Shaktipat probably want to do it as fast as possible because the longer the duration, the more things can go wrong and you might lose your concentration. As soon as it's available, you pray to the Guru and block off the eight lower gates. If the Guru knows that you're dying, he'll come to the physical place and just make sure everything is OK and "whoooosh" pull you out. But it's not necessary that the Guru be physically present because it's a consciousness thing. It's best if the Guru knows and can practice the blocking of the eight gates and the phowa.

Basically you're going straight from incarnation in a body straight into enlightenment and the Clear Light. From that point you can either be absorbed or you can be guided to a yogic paradise. That's the thing these days. It used to be an absorption thing, but now what is in vogue is you'll be sent to a yogic paradise where you'll gain yogic skills and increase your skills of Samadhi and then reincarnate and do some kind of service in the body and express realization physically. It's up to you; it's not necessary. You can merge then if you want.

If the Guru is out of the body it won't matter because

you've formed a relationship with the Guru. The Guru is the Great Light inside the body but once he drops the body, he's still the Great Light. I'll stress this again. One of the aspects of studying with the Guru is learning the art of communication. My Guru died twenty some years ago, but I'd gotten really good at psychic contact with him when he was alive and then after he dropped his body, contact actually got easier because he had no limitation. It doesn't get harder; it gets easier. He's in a Siddhaloka kind of plane; it's an ecstatic plane. That gives you the ability to merge with an ecstatic plane of consciousness. It makes it easier. All of you have that full benefit of the lineage at the moment of death.

The Bardo Thodol puts an underline under phowa. This is the best way because not only do you have your skill going for you but you also have the skill of the Guru and the force of the lineage behind you. So we're all learning and we have X amount of skill and what skill we don't have, the Guru makes up for and will not allow you under any circumstance to be lost in the Bardo.

Remember the seat of the Guru at the crown of the head. Call the Guru to that seat. Merge. Remember that the Bodhicitta is at the seat of the heart and in the brain – the Red and White essence of the Bodhicitta merge at the heart. That's you. That's the essence of you. That's interesting because the point of infusion where the mystery of life infuses into the physical form takes place at the crown of the head. What I understand is that the Great Light is like a vortex there. It churns the milk of the universe and produces an atmosphere and that's the White Bodhicitta. The drop of the Red Bodhicitta is the SO mantra and the White Bodhicitta is the HAM mantra. Bring them together and merge up through the brain and exit. You'll go instantly into the ocean of consciousness. That's why you always want to keep the relationship with the Guru completely open and clear. You don't want complexity between you at that moment. It is a guarded relationship. It is virtually foolproof. But again, it's a tricky moment and you have to have the presence of mind when you start to see the symptoms of death. It's best to be prepared. Even if it's just going to be very quick, you'll have an hour or so to pull yourself together, that's all you'll need. That's why it's a little more complicated with sudden deaths, accidents, plane crashes and those kinds of things. They produce a maelstrom of events that can be confusing though not insurmountable. But hopefully your spiritual life will unfold the karmic knots that will produce such a death. One of the best forms of good karma is that you have a couple of minutes to pull yourself together before you make the leap.

So that deals with the Chikhai Bardo and the beginning of the Chonyid Bardo and the phowa, the transference of consciousness.

Let's do a quick recap. The Bardo Thodol, which liberates upon contact, presents three possibilities:

1. Direct Recognition of the Clear Light
2. Phowa
3. The 100 Fibers – Spontaneously Enlightened and Their Contact is Spontaneously Enlightening

The superior way is the direct recognition of the nature of the Clear Light as empty, recognizing that both life and death arise simultaneously and are empty – that it's only the Clear Light that is present. You should understand that the superior path is present at every stage of the Bardo. Any one point is a Chikhai Bardo of the face-to-face with the Clear Light and the collapsing of the elements one into another. If one recognizes at any point that they are empty, that the Clear Light is the only reality, the Bardo collapses and enlightenment is achieved.

The middle path is the path of the phowa, the nine

gates. This is also a form of Chöd, the transference of consciousness directly into the Clear Light, directly into the ocean of consciousness from the Bardo of Life. This recognizes that each of the nine gates, each of the holes of the body, is a pathway into a different realm, and that by willfully controlling the gate out of which one exits the body, one can guarantee enlightenment – specifically by exiting out through the hole at the crown of the head. This can be done by anyone through yogic skill. It's not that hard to do. One simply needs the presence of mind to do it. If one has a connection with the Guru, that connection virtually guarantees this outcome. Although when you're dealing with the Bardo, anything can happen and everything needs to be dealt with very seriously.

The understanding of the nine gates is: The gate of the anus is the gateway to the Bardo of Hell. The gateway of the genital region is the gateway into the animal realm. The navel is the gateway to the desire or jealous gods. The gateway of the mouth is the pathway of the hungry ghost, the preta. The nose is the gateway of the human realms. The eyes are the form realms of the gods. The forehead, between the eyebrows, are the formless realms of the gods. And the crown at the top of the head is the gateway into the ocean of consciousness. (See Diagram.)

Thus we see the practice of pranayama, the control of the breath and the alignment of the consciousness with the space between the breaths, the importance of raising Bodhicitta and the importance of the Pratyahara, all of which will aid in the phowa, the transference of consciousness at the moment of death. This is the great gift of the Bardo Thodol. The author, Padmasambhava, recommends the phowa as your best chance to get enlightenment at death.

So now we've dealt with the Chikhai Bardo and the opening of the Chonyid Bardo, the condition where the consciousness emerges out of the three days of absorption into the Great Light, where having refused to merge, the beginning of the karmic conditions ensues. We've also addressed the phowa, which is the advised way to exit the body. It can be done by anyone with even a little bit of experience and will, even if the person does not have a Guru but comes into contact with this methodology, and has learned to absorb the consciousness into the central nerve, to block off the lower eight gates and to move consciousness out through the crown of the head. If you have a Guru, call on the Guru at the moment of the Great Light and the Guru will aid in the blocking off of the eight lower gates and put the extra spiritual force on the attraction of your consciousness principle at the crown of the head.

Once that is accomplished, you will merge directly into the Great Light and be liberated.

At any moment, by recognizing the empty nature of reality the Bardo collapses and enlightenment occurs. This is what is called 'recognition'. It is the superior way. The combination of recognition and phowa is very efficient.

Next we will deal with the arising of the peaceful and wrathful deities, the 100 fibers and the pathway of rebirth.

Now if having failed at the moment of the Chikhai and the Great Light and the phowa has not been completely fulfilled, then the Chonyid begins to develop. Now it's important to understand that in all of these cases, more spiritual training will buy you the ability to pull yourself together so that at any given moment you can recognize the nature of the Clear Light in the manifestations of what are taking place in the Bardo dream and you become liberated at that moment.

If you are in the Bardo at this point, what has happened is that you have had conflicting desires and even terror, and taken flight. At this time you have come face to face with the Great Light and you have mistaken the Great Light for something fearful or destructive of your identity, taken the false refuge in the belief of an individual existence in the body and held to the apparition.

There's a quality of reality that we call 'The Three Worlds' that takes place in what is represented as the OM: The *Dharmakaya*, the *Shambogakaya* and the *Nirmanakaya*. The Dharmakaya is pure light. The Shambogakaya is pure energy. The Nirmanakaya is pure form. Each state of the Bardo reflects one of the three worlds. The Chikhai Bardo reflects the Dharmakaya. The Chonyid Bardo reflects the Shambogakaya. The Sidpa Bardo represents the Nirmanakaya. They are the Bardos of consciousness, energy and form. Any of the three are still advents into the Great Light but they are different pathways that are progressing.

THE 100 FIBERS OF THE CHONYID

We have discussed the collapse of the elemental basis of reality – earth into water; earth and water into fire; earth, water and fire into air; earth, water, fire and air into ether – and the experience of the Great Light in the greater and lesser forms, and the phowa.

The manifestation that begins now is the beginning of the unfoldment of the 100 fibers that takes place in fourteen days. The 100 spontaneously enlightened deities are the 100 fibers that flow from the six chakras. So now we're dealing with the exact quality of the Bardo Thodol – the entire ida, pingala and sushumna are illuminated and the elemental chakras of earth, water, fire, air and ether, are now beginning to manifest and they begin to appear in your Bardo dream as the onset of the appearance of the lights of the Bardo.

The qualities of the lights of the Bardo on days one through seven are the 42 pacific or peaceful deities. They are quiescent and luminous. On the eighth day the manifestation of the 58 wrathful deities occurs. The peaceful deities are the fibers that originate in the heart aspect of the Bodhicitta and the wrathful deities are the fibers that originate in the mind aspect of the Bodhicitta. Remember that we also call the Bodhicitta the heart-mind.

The White Bodhicitta is the HAM; the Red Bodhicitta is the SO. If at this point you have failed to recognize the Great Light, the Clear Light of Reality, then the lights of the Bardo begin and the dawning of the peaceful deities. You'll be experiencing the attraction and repulsion at each of these lights but at any point if you were to realize that they were the arising of the Clear Light of Reality, the light would disappear and you would be liberated.

On the first day the appearance of a dull white light manifests simultaneously with a brilliant blue light. The dull white light is the manifestation of the deva worlds, the manifestation of jealous gods and form gods. The brilliant blue light is the light of the Dharmakaya, the light of dharma, of the higher intuition, pure aspects of mind and high philosophical thought. In this case the light to select is the brilliant blue light. If you recognize the brilliant blue light as the light of the Dharmakaya, you'll go directly into the Dharmakaya. This is the first day.

On the second day there is the manifestation of a dull smoky light and a bright white light. The dull smoky light is the manifestation of the Bardo of Hell. The bright white light is the light of wisdom or skillful means. It is the manifestation of the Vajrapani, the skillful means. They will come to you and you will see them as the karmic condition, the karmic content of your thought-constructs, that will play out in the colors of the lights. It is one of the archetypes of the awakened mind. Dull, smoky is hell realm. Everyone repeat after me…"Dull, smoky, bad," (Laughter) until you're a Bodhisattva and then you can do what you want.

On the third day, the manifestation of the dazzling yellow light, which is the second form of wisdom, and a dull blue light appear. The dull blue light is the human plane. Again, the dazzling yellow light is a paradise. When we're talking about wisdom, we're dealing with a realm of paradise. It's a loka of pure light, pure consciousness and it is a reappearance of the wisdom frequency. The dull blue light is the plane of humans and the human spirit so you'll go to the realm of the human as well as the ghosts of humans.

On the fourth day, a brilliant red light will appear and this is the light of the fire element. At the same time a dull, dim red light will be manifesting, which is the preta-loka, the world of hungry ghosts.

On the fifth day a brilliant green light will appear. This is the element of water. At the same time a dim green light, which is the light of the world of the jealous gods, will appear.

On the sixth day you will see a manifestation of multiple lights of yellow, green, red, white and blue. These are the assembled manifestation of the entire field of elements, earth, water, fire, air and ether. At this point all 42 of the peaceful deities will manifest. They will appear in their forms as lights. They will also appear in their personalities and as the expression of your karmic content. As I said, these aspects of the Bardo are the same for everybody. You should also understand that all of these elements are your own thought-constructs, so based on conditioning and training, you will animate the appearance of the deities. Because there is a part of the reflex of mind that is in formation, a part of the reflex of mind that is in vibration, and a part of the reflex of the mind that is in consciousness, your mind will fill in the blanks. It will give these lights colors, formation and personalities. They will ask you questions, interact with you and they will produce dreams according to the corollary of their component content. Because at this point in the Bardo, if you are still in the Bardo it means that you have an attachment to your karmic conditions. The karmic conditions that are aligned along the 100 fibers of the 50 male and 50 female deities will behave in ways that express your karmic content in each of these areas.

It's interesting as you begin to advance in your meditation you begin to go through all the states of the Bardo. You see the god realms, you see the jealous god realms, you see the human realms, you see the hell realms, you see the preta realms, and they tend to be in the colors of these lights. You can tell when there's no color that you're glancing through or coming into contact with the Hell realm. It's all dull grays and blacks. The deva realm is a kind of infinite white light that pervades everything. The Dharmakaya is a brilliant blue light. It's called *citi*, the scintillating light of consciousness. The fire element is red and so all of the karma inside of the fire element is at the navel – that is a position of will. All of the karma that is connected with the fibers of the will produce a quality of dreams. It's as though those dreams all have a red gel on them; there's a red cast to everything.

The next thing that will appear are the lights of the six lokas, which are the god realm, jealous god realm, human realm, preta realm, plants and animals and Hell realm and they will be in the various colors of the elements.

On the seventh day, at the end of the manifestation of the 42 peaceful deities, is the famous Judgment. This is the point where the karmic content of all of the fibers of consciousness release their content into the brain and every single instant of your incarnation is played out. As I said, when you look at a subtle body, the dark negative karma appears as a kind of piece of black tar sitting in the subtle body. The good karma looks like a bright little white piece of rice, but small, like a grain of salt.

The Judgment is the absolute mathematical weight and balance of good and bad karma that is the presence of the full force of the five elements. At this moment you will experience with excruciating detail the seed of every action. You'll feel your karma arising as the weight of your judgment as a system and it will move you into the next day.

The moment of the Judgment produces a mechanical movement into the second stage of the manifestation of the 100 deities and this is the beginning of the 58 wrathful deities. They are characterized as the blood-drinking deities. They are very fierce, very dramatic, very intense and very swift because they carry the nature of the speed of mind. The pivot point is the seventh day where the Judgment has occurred, where you assess the weights and balances of your own karma, the full weight and balance of every good and bad action. If you accept that judgment, that produces the movement into the eighth day and this is the beginning of a kind of anguishing phase where the 58 wrathful deities are very swift and very terrifying.

All of the dynamics of the unconscious, of the subconscious unconscious, of our subconscious and unconscious basic human brain, and of the lizard brain, the primordial aspect of the lizard brain that is the brain pre-conscience, pre-reason, that is still present inside the brain, inside the mind, are all part of the 58 wrathful deities. And there is an even deeper brain that is the limbic region, the sheer survival with no development of the higher angels. At the same time they will manifest as the six overarching lobes of the brain and you will be dealing with a balance and equilibrium of the conscious, subconscious, unconscious component of your mind, the lizard mind and the primordial limbic mind. They tend to characterize themselves in the forms of light producing images that are very ferocious. As I said, they are characterized as the blood-drinking deities.

The reason that you are at this stage in the Bardo is because of your attachment to an identity and your belief in an "I". Even at this point you will have a thought-mind-body that will be operating as an identity and it will be you. You'll assemble yourself in some mental picture. But because of your attachment to the belief in an "I", the 58 wrathful deities will manifest with a great intensity. The reason that you are still in the Bardo at this point, having failed to recognize the Clear Light, having had limited response with the phowa, is because you're still clinging to an identity which means that you are afflicted with a deep form of ignorance, so the wrathful identities attack the ignorance itself and they take the form of blood-drinking monstrous forms.

The primordial mind is the fight or flight mind and so it exists in a condition of total fear on the trigger of existence or nonexistence. The lizard mind, the saurian mind, the first form of life, is a form of mind that existed before the existence of a conscience or a reason. So all of that content is there and it dumps, it releases and it tends to take on those kinds of forms. There is a manifestation of fierce forms, frightening sounds and ever-increasingly violent, afflictive dream signs in the apparition of the dream Bardo. But what is interesting is at the end of the seventh day, the 42 peaceful deities manifest and then the Judgment occurs. The entire weight of all the karma strikes the mind and the brain just processes it like a raw algorithm. If you accept that algorithm, that's the Judgment and then the force of the 58 wrathful deities begin to act upon your acceptance of your own judgment and you produce the positive and negative unfoldment of the next seven days of the arising of the wrathful deities, which attack the ignorance itself. But it is you, yourself who identified with the ignorance and so you feel that you, yourself are being attacked. You're not at all. All of the energies of the wrathful deities are spontaneously enlightened forms that are seeking to expiate the accepted judgment of the accumulated karma. But because you failed to recognize the truth of the Clear Light inside the Judgment, which is an immediate release, you live out the Judgment in the next eight days.

The first manifestation of the wrathful deities is

actually a form of grace. On the eighth day, again there will be a manifestation of the appearance of the divine light. It will be the Clear Light of Reality. It will take the form of God manifesting as a God form. Whatever is within your system will be selected by the mind and presented to you. It will also present the Guru to you. The Guru is a reflex of God. The Guru is not a person or a place or a thing. The Guru is an eternal spirit that arises at the beginning of creation and exists as the agency of liberation and mercy. So God will arise as the Guru. This could be a manifestation of Dorje Chang or a manifestation like Shiva – it will be a universal form. It will also be very awesome.

Once we hit the wrathful deities, everything takes on a very awesome aspect – a very fearful, overwhelming, off-the-charts kind of quality. The first manifestation of the eighth day is God in the form of liberation in the form of the Guru. Everybody here will have an incredibly awesome appearance of Shiva. If you manage to accept the grace of the wrathful form of God, your sins are wiped away and you are liberated right there.

On the ninth day the manifestation of the blood-drinking deities manifests. This is a very ferocious onslaught of the subconscious and unconscious reflexes of Vajra anger, Vajra lust, Vajra greed and Vajra envy. They are the underlying energies at the primal level – very intense, very terrifying. Again, if you're able to think of the Guru and recognize him as the Clear Light of Reality, they will dissolve and you'll be liberated.

On the tenth day, a very intense yellow light will arise. This is the beginning of the manifestation of the mind-essence. This is a form of compassion, one of the highest angels of the expression of love. But because it is in the wrathful stage, it will again be like a blazing sun. At this point we don't get oppositions; we just get great singularities. We're not dealing with positive or negative; they will just be these great singular energies with very intense personalities.

The eleventh day is the will to live. It's called *padma*. It is a form of existence; it is the essence of nature. It is the primal force of life itself. It will be a brilliant light that is dark reddish in color and will take the form of a lotus. This is the crown of the twelve Mothers at the crown of the head.

If you remember when we were studying the Shiva Sutras, again the numbers of the alphabet of the petals of the lotus are 50 in number, so there are 50 fibers that operate the 100 fibers – 50 male fibers and 50 female fibers, each one a syllable, an element of the alphabet that is called the *malini*. As each of the fibers that flows from the chakras assemble and disassemble, it's like taking the alphabet and beginning to form words. That is the concept of the matrika.

So the padma rises up into the upper brain and there's a lotus with twelve petals in the upper brain and they are the ruling energies of the 50 syllables of the alphabet that are right on the petals. And what you're seeing is the architecture of reality being constructed. This is the Bardo Thodol, the interval, being stripped down to its essence. This is the holy dharma unfolding. You're getting to this point where you bypass the personal karmic conditions. It will still manifest in terms of your karma conditions, but the ruling quality will be the twelve Mothers that rule the 50.

On the twelfth day a dark green light will appear and this is the energy of karma. The power of karma is the power of cause and effect, the equilibrium of cause and effect. This is the principle of infinite polarity between the red and the white lights of the Bodhicitta manifesting as the male and female principle. Cause and effect are eternally wedded and the principle of their infinite connection is karma. It will be a dark green light and it will arise out of infinite creation.

On the thirteenth day the *kerimas* will arise from the brain. The kerimas are the animal forces. They are the subconscious and unconscious wrathful forces, the lizard brain and the qualities of the primitive levels of the brain and mind formation. They will come in the form of animals or terrifying beings with animal heads and then you will know that you are dealing with the limbic and saurian brain. They are very terrifying and they are void. They arise empty; they arise as void. If you were to recognize their void nature as the Clear Light of Reality, you would be liberated at that moment.

On the fourteenth day there is an assault of the entire order of the 58 wrathful deities with 30 wrathful male forms and 28 wrathful female forms. They will arrive in the full aura of colors, everywhere from black, smoky black, white, red, green, yellow, blue and in-between tones which are the full aurora of the wrathful deities. They will emerge from the quadrants of the brain.

During this entire time it is important to understand that these are all forms of the Dharmaraja, the manifestation of death as the Clear Light of Reality. They are your own thought-constructs. They're not monsters coming to destroy you. They are the constructs of your own mind. They've always been there. The drama of the moment of death is that the buffering and filtering of the conditional layers of physical, subtle physical and mental bodies is removed and everything is experienced with its absolute essence.

Once you learn to eliminate the fear, the Bardo is a very interesting experience. At this point your being is a form of thought. You are a thought-body. Because you're still existing in the Bardo, there's a fear reflex and thus you are still of the form of desire. What is happening is a kind of hallucination but it will be very real to you. One of the reasons why I say that life and death are the same is that the appearance of the world is also a hallucination – all of this. This is the basis of emptiness. There is no object-ness to the appearance of the world. It is a reflex of consciousness taking place in the perceiver. If the world were real, everyone would see the same thing. The fact that it is in flux shows that it arises as a chemical reaction of consciousness to form.

The Judgment is a mirror. Exactly every moment, every instant of your existence is weighed and broken down into an algorithm. If you accept it, you accept the Judgment. If you see it as pure light you are liberated. Throughout this time it is important to stay calm. Do not be thrown by the horrific side of the manifestations. You will find that it's very easy to do that if you remember to recognize that you are the Clear Light. The medicine at any given moment is to remember the Guru. If you call for the Guru at any point in this process, the Guru will come, stabilize you and give you your best chance to awaken, to see the unfoldment of the Bardo as void and empty. Always remember the overwhelming influence of thought. Especially in the Bardo, what you think is what happens. In other words, if you think about a demon that is going to come and eat you, a demon will come and eat you. This is the same way in life but it seems to be more distant.

We've gone through the fourteen days during which the 42 peaceful deities and the 58 wrathful deities will have manifested. At this point if you have failed to recognize the Clear Light of Reality in the manifestation of the 100 spontaneously enlightened deities, the appearance of the lights of the six lokas will take place. At which time you will have come to the end of the Chonyid Bardo having gone through day one through fourteen, having experienced the Judgment. You are still in the Bardo, having failed to recognize the Clear Light.

CHAPTER 6

SIDPA BARDO

The next manifestation is the Wheel of Six Lights. These are the lights of the Six Realms of Transitory Existence. They will manifest as: a Great White Light – this light is the light of the god realm; a red light is the light of the jealous gods; a green light is the light of the animal realm; a yellow light is the light of the pretas, the hungry ghosts; a dark, smoky light is the light of hell; and a blue light is the light of human existence. They will appear simultaneously in a wheel. (See diagram).

At this point, having failed to recognize the Clear Light, you are now on track for reincarnation and rebirth. Each of these lights representing the god realms, jealous gods, animals, hungry ghost, and human are open to you like a doorway.

At this time your thought formation will change. By the time you go through the attack of the 52 wrathful deities, your ability to assemble yourself as yourself will be gone. You will have lost memory of yourself. You'll no longer be you. You will be a consciousness principle being buffeted around by the unbridled forms of consciousness that are the onslaught of the wrathful deities. What they do is they basically strip you down of everything. This is the point where you lose your memory of your previous life. This is why nobody can remember what they were before.

You will now start to manifest as elemental energies and the karmic tendencies of the Bardo will begin to assert themselves. You will begin to catch a vision of the qualities of your next life. If your future is in the god realms, you'll see beautiful gardens. If your future existence is going to be in the realm of the jealous gods, you'll see a cave. You'll appear in a cave if your existence is going to be in the animal realm. If you're going to be a preta, you'll manifest inside a pile of burning wood. If you're going to manifest in Hell, you'll see yourself inside a black house with red trim. You'll also fold through the realities. You might feel yourself to be a bundle of reeds or a tree or some kind of assembly of nature. If you're going to be in the human realm, you'll tend to see a kind of serenity – houses, fields, signs of agriculture and organized architecture. At this point it is possible to meditate on God and the Guru, generate the phowa, recognize the Clear Light of Reality and be liberated.

As you're drawn through the selected Bardo of your future life, you'll begin to see visions of your future incarnation. First thing you'll see on the human incarnation, is again, organized architecture. It's one of the signs of human existence. You'll come through a doorway inside the Bardo – it gets very difficult to describe – you'll be attracted into one of these lights. Once you become a human, it is difficult to descend, so you'll be attracted to the blue light. You'll be drawn into the blue light and you'll pull through the blue light of the wheel of psychic existence into the human realm.

As you approach the human realm you'll begin to see an array of continents as if they were islands floating in the sky. There are four continents that are organized into the four directions – southern continent, eastern continent, northern continent and western continent. (See diagram).

If it's the southern continent, you will signs of beautiful houses and agriculture. The southern continent is desirable because on the southern continent you will live a very rich life. You will live a life of ease and wealth, along with the presence of dharma.

On the eastern continent you will see very beautiful people, beautiful men and women. You will also see beautiful people gathered around a lake – very young and healthy. This is a beautiful heavenly life, but not desirable because there is little or no dharma on the eastern continent.

On the western continent you will see horses – beautiful stallions and mares gathering around the lake. It is a beautiful life but no dharma.

On the northern continent you will see beautiful gardens, beautiful lakes and mountains. In this continent your life will be beautiful, but there is not the presence of dharma.

You want to seek the southern continent with its beautiful houses and signs of agriculture. This has the totally enriched human life. This is the human existence where you are certain to come into contact with dharma – blue light –> human realm –> look for beautiful houses with signs of agriculture and a beautiful lake. Houses are the key.

As you select this continent you will then see your

future mother and father in the act of making love. In the male incarnation you will be attracted to the mother; if your incarnation is going to be female, you will be attracted to the father. This is the manifestation of the zygote, the fertilized egg in the beginning of the movement through the womb gate. At this point if you were to recognize the manifestation of the continents' psychic existence as the Clear Light of Reality, you would be liberated and not be reborn.

One of the manifestations of the consciousness as it moves between life and death is characterized in spiritual thought as a red-hot iron bar, which symbolizes existence. When it is in the interval state, the Thodol state, the intermediate condition, it is red-hot and flexible. Steel is malleable and can be moved into multiple shapes. As it moves closer and closer into the rebirth, the steel cools and becomes rigid. At this point you experience a severe ramping down of opportunities – selection of the human realm, selection of the continent of human existence, selection of the mother and father.

At this point everything happens very quickly. You have now selected the mother and father. Their union, their copulation will produce the fertilized egg. That is the first form of the new incarnation.

The movement of the egg into the womb is the last stage of the Bardo. At this point the iron bar is becoming very cool and rigid. All of the selectivity has been made – the place, the time, the qualities of the mother and father that will be transferred to the child – and the womb gate is set.

There is given a last opportunity to escape the Bardo in a series of opportunities called 'closing the womb door'. If at this point, even as you arise as the fertilized egg, you meditate on God and the Guru, you can stop thought, recognize the Clear Light and the womb gate will be closed. This actually happens a lot. You will see people in the last stages of rebirth and one soul after another is moving through an egg. When you see a female who is about to be impregnated, you'll see lots of souls looming around in her mind-space, all seeking the womb gate. There's a quality of pressure wherein even in the last moment a realization can take place. If one meditates on God and the Guru, the womb gate will be shut and one is liberated. That soul simply vacates the egg and another soul will enter the new space.

Meditation on God; meditation on the Guru, either one. Stopping thought and recognizing the Clear Light of Reality. By meditating on the Guru and praying to the Guru that the womb gate be closed, based on your connection with the Guru, that boon can be gained wherein you'll have a new opportunity for the phowa, stop the womb gate, merge with the Guru, merge with the Clear Light of Reality and attain liberation. We're back to the very beginning. Recognize that life, birth and death are the same. They are void, an empty dream. Even as you've gone through the gate of death, you've traversed the entire interval of the intermediate state and are now standing at the gate of rebirth. If at that moment you realize that death, life and rebirth are void/empty and of the nature of the Clear Light, liberation arises.

This is the last opportunity one has. If you can relax and calm the mind and allow the mind to go into the natural condition - at this stage, because it's unformed into the new personality - it can slide into the natural state and arise as the Clear Light. Again, meditate on the Guru.

If one has been faced with the entire traversing of the Bardo, some 49 days have taken place. It is possible to arrange to have the Bardo Thodol text recited continuously for the entire 49 days. At any one moment while you're in the maelstrom of the Bardo, if you can hear the words of truth, your mind will reverse its position of being entranced in the Bardo, recognize the Clear Light, and liberation will be achieved.

All forms of the selection of birth, such as supernatural birth by arising of mind, egg birth (animal), womb birth (human, mammal) and sweat birth (insect) carry the Clear Light. And they are all subject to ability and to karma. The higher path (such as supernatural birth by arising of mind) is based on greater ability and positive karma. The lower path, having traversed the entire Chikhai, the entire Chonyid, the entire Sidpa, is of lesser ability, more afflictive karma. But the two major factors of the entire process are the process of karmic conditions and connections, which means the Guru.

Connections to a spiritual authority can produce a level of performance that you would not have a hope of doing on your own. It's like a spiritual boost. The Guru presents himself at the beginning of the eighth day. God in the form of the Guru appears to you after you've just been judged. The Guru will appear to you again in the form of the Guru and he'll say, "This is all a dream." Recognize the Guru as the form of the Great Clear Light and you're out. The Guru will continually come to you inside the Bardo and try to snap you out of it at every stage. Grace, which is an unearned or unasked for favor, is a gift that will come to you. The quality of the liberation will be attenuated to the abilities, to the karma and to the dynamic connections. It is possible through the grace of the Guru that you can gain the realization of the Dharmakaya, appear in the Clear Light and move to a chain of existence in yogic paradise. It's like having a family connection that gets you into Harvard. Your grades are so-so, but somebody kicks a door open for you. Happens all the time. Happens all the time in the world, happens all the time in the Bardo.

Otherwise the next thing that happens is the womb gate. You're grasped by one claw and with a smack on the ass the first roar of Rudra occurs. (Laughter)

Thank you very much. This path cannot fail to grant liberation.

Victory to all Gurus. Om Swaha

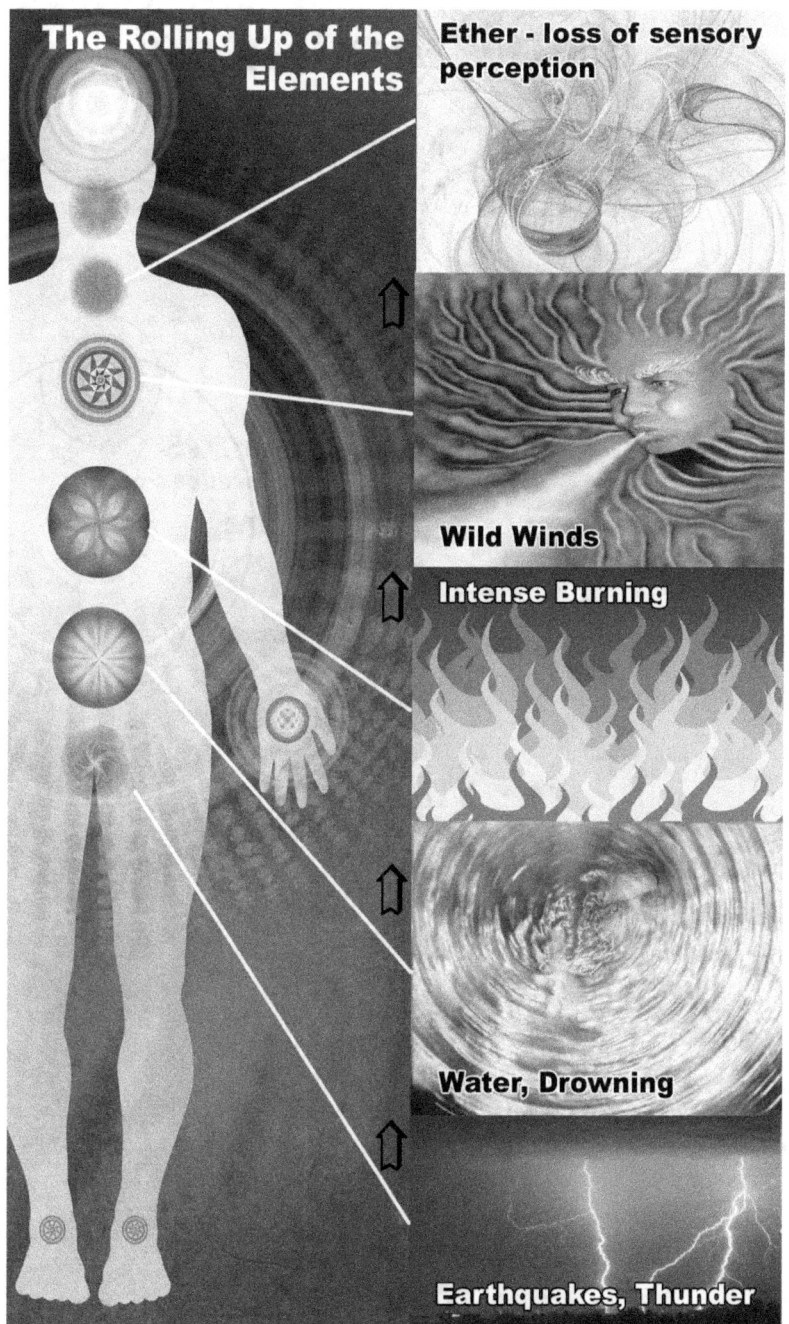

The Bardo Thodol ~ 103

Days 1-7 ... The 42 Peaceful Deities

Light of Dharma (Dharmakaya)	**Day 1**	Devas Gods
Skillful Means (Vajrapani)	**Day 2**	Hell
Wisdom	**Day 3**	Human
Discrimination	**Day 4**	Preta
Action	**Day 5**	Jealous Gods

Day 6

earth • water • fire • air • ether

ELEMENTS　　　　　**LOKAS**

God • Jealous God • Human • Preta • Plants/Animals • Hell

Day 7　　The Judgment

The Bardo Thodol ~ 106

Days 8-14 ... The 58 Wrathful Deities

Day 8 — **Clear Light of Reality God / Guru**

Day 9 — **Blood Drinking Deities**

Day 10 — **Mind Essence Compassion**

Day 11 — **Padma Will to Live**

Day 12 — **Karma**

Day 13 — **Kerimas Animal Forces**

Day 14 — **All 58 Wrathful Deities**

The Wheel of Six Lights
Doorways into the Six Realms of
Transitory Existence and Rebirth

Devas - gods, though not immortal or omniscient
Asuras - demigods or jealous gods
Pretas - hungry ghosts

The Four Continents

Mountains, Gardens and Lakes

Horses and Lakes

Beautiful People and Lakes

Agriculture and Architecture
~ and DHARMA

The Bardo Thodol ~ 109

The Three Stages of the Bardo Thodol

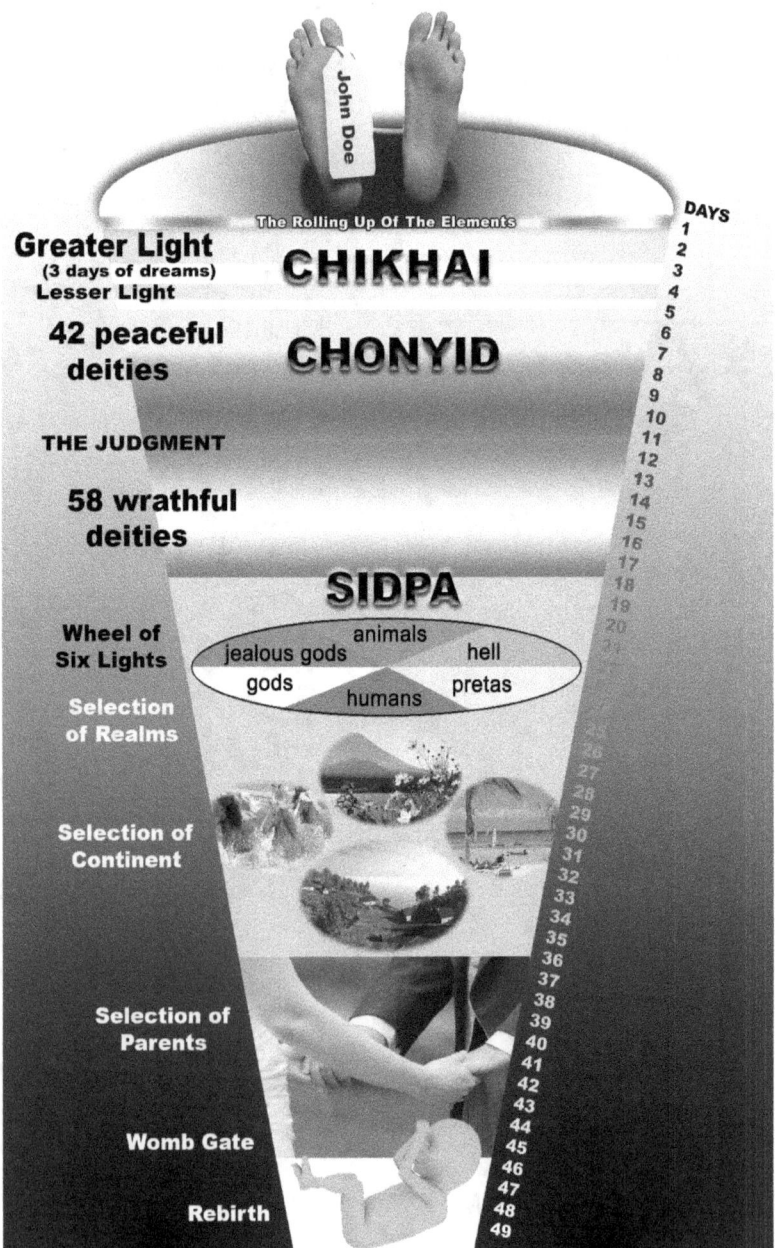

CHAPTER 7

QUESTIONS AND ANSWERS

Question: Does the Clear Light ever look like a rainbow?

Mark: Yes. There is a phase when the Clear Light merges into the mind and all five lights appear at once. It is multi-hued and this is in the phase of the 100 deities, when the 100 fibers are manifesting, when the 100 fibers merge into the brain, manifesting as a rainbow. Again, there is the possibility when the Clear Light arises, if one has missed the first opportunity of the Clear Light, the red bindu of the Red Bodhicitta and the white bindu of the White Bodhicitta can be brought to the center. You should understand that the Red and White Bodhicitta are the Clear Light manifesting inside the mind-body. Meditate on them with deep abandon. You'll merge into the Clear Light and you'll exit the Bardo.

Question: Is it important that during these three to seven days someone be present with the body?

Mark: If a person is of little or no training, they will find the presence of a companion or a loved one soothing, so yes, that's valuable. It's also valuable that a person can be read the text from the Bardo Thodol. While they're in the state, you can read it to them in any language and they will understand it because it is of a divine origin and you are speaking directly to the mind essence. The person won't be intellectually mulling it over; they will experience the expression of the Bardo directly. I would say that most people, because they're going into the great unknown, would be comforted by the presence of a loved one. It's bittersweet because they're comforted by their presence but they're leaving them never to return.

Question: I have a couple of questions about how the American process interferes with this whole thing. I've seen people pass and then somebody shows up in a car with a stretcher and they put the body on the stretcher and take them away.

Mark: I think that's one of the most important preparations. If you become the keeper and caretaker of a person's body while they're going through the death process, you should exert your power to give them those three days. It will be better.

Question: How do you do that legally? Is there a way to legally say that to the system, to the hospital, to the mortician?

Mark: What I would do is just not make the phone call until the third day is up. If death is inevitable, hospitals will gladly let you go die at home. It's much better to die at home. Hospitals are a nightmare. If a person is manifesting the symptoms of death, then this thing is inevitable. Just take them home and put them in their surroundings because when they go into the death condition, they become hyper aware of the surroundings of their body. Hospitals are completely zones of total suffering. You become intensely aware of the anguish of hundreds if not thousands of people. It would be disturbing to your mind. It's very important.

Question: In Chikhai does the Great Light appear at the same time as all the desires are happening? Is that what is so difficult?

Mark: What resists the Great Light is the attachment to the desire body of the individual life. You still think you're a body and you still think there's a chance that you're going to be able to keep your body and you misunderstand the approach of the Great Light as something that is going to destroy your life, destroy your connection to your body. It is indeed and so you're right about that, but there's not the slightest chance that you're going to keep your body. But out of misunderstanding people will hope, even at that moment, to try and hang on to the body and all it represents. It's a false refuge. That's why I say it's a misunderstanding. The approach of the Great Light is something of great auspiciousness and an opportunity for enlightenment. Right there. Even if you didn't do a single ounce of spiritual training, but you understood that the Great Light was God, you could merge with God at that moment and it would be over. You'd be enlightened.

Question: So it's not desire that is the problem, it's the desire for the body and for life, in essence?

Mark: Which makes desire the problem. The mistake is that desire produces a form of ignorance that causes you to generate a form of action.

Question: Does the Great Light then appear as the image of Jesus for some people or is it always the ten billion suns?

Mark: It's the Great Light; it is formless. But you can condition yourself to know that when the Great Light comes, it's going to be my God. Whatever your image of God will be, it will work because it's all the same thing. That's the ridiculous point of the ride of religions. It's all going to the same place.

Question: I was thinking if the Christians got to see the Great Light as Jesus, then they would get an unfair advantage on this test. My seeing it as a billion suns seems like the scarier than hell presentation of God as opposed to seeing it as a human personified form. But nobody sees it in the human personified form.

Mark: What you do is you prepare your mind by saying that you're about to meet God and whatever is your God – fill in your blank – when that Great Light comes, you have prepared yourself to know that "It's God and I won't be afraid. I will be awestruck, I will be humble and I will accept that light. I won't run." So it's valuable. Most of the time if a person has had good karma, they'll perhaps have a little bit of time to prepare. If their life is religious, they'll go to that recourse of whatever that personality is. And that's the best thing to do because it calms the mind and heart. The mind is basically shattered by the Great Light. You're absorbed. A personification will keep your mind and heart calm until that moment and hopefully when it happens it 's kind of a moment of faith. If you really believe that your God is God, then as it happens you'll be at peace and you won't be afraid and it will work.

Question: The last time you talked about this, you gave the exact same speech and we were sitting on top of a mountain at Kennedy Meadows and I was thinking to myself, "This is no sweat, all I gotta do is just think that this is God and move to it and this sounds like it's totally manageable ("It is", says Mark) and you talked about it being the ten billion suns and how formidable and intense and tremendous this power is that is going to be in front of you and at the exact point that you talked about this on the mountain, one of these jet fighters – an F16 or something – flew directly over us and the sound and the fury of that engine as it flew over us scared the living hell out of me, to the point where I said if I am so frightened of this plane flying overhead, how the hell am I ever going to manage the ten billion suns that are going to light up in front of me?

Mark: And that is the question. Because it's just everything; it's beyond comprehension, beyond whatever you expect it to be.

Question: That's because you don't set us up for it. You say "Oh, it will just be a light that you will just go to." (Laughter)

Mark: Well, it's better to always present things in a positive way. (Laughter)

Question: That gave me the clue of what the heck was really going on when I felt that plane. If I'm scared of this, there's no way – I'm going to run like hell.

Mark: And that's what everybody does. That's why there are so many people. (Laughter)

Question: You said that we have several chances for the Clear Light of Eternity. ("100", says Mark) 100 chances? I thought you said it was 100 fibers?

Mark: Each fiber is a chance that presents an opportunity to recognize the fiber as the Clear Light of Reality.

Question: So you mean that at the same time that the fiber is unloading or downloading that vibe, the Clear Light is also present at the same time?

Mark: Yes!

Question: Oh my gosh, I didn't realize that. Wow, so there's a split screen where you've got two different things going on ("And you go either way", says Mark) and nobody ever runs to the light when these demonic apparitions are showing?

Mark: That's the thing. They get thrown into a progressive hysteria.

Question: And then the light is a different color as this progresses?

Mark: There are a series of color changes of light because the different fibers are different combinations of the elements, the different fibers – ida, pingala and sushumna, elemental basis, etc. Some manifest as all of the lights at once, all five lights, some of them are yellow, some are blue, some are dominant. You'll always get a dominant and a sub-dominant light, a lesser or greater, and it will tend to be that the dominant light is the positive light, the Clear Light manifesting as the good quality, and as we go down the chain, you're going deeper and deeper into the Bardo, so it's more and more murky on the Bardo side and more difficult to recognize the Clear Light. The dominant light tends to be the light that represents the Clear Light and there will be a lesser light at each point. In other words, it's the SO and the HAM. The SO, the Creation and the HAM, the ocean of infinite consciousness. It will come at you in sets of two.

Question: I always thought that there were different lights and some lights we were supposed to ignore and stay away from and some we're supposed to go towards. What you're saying then is basically go toward whatever light shows up at any time during these 100 fibers?

Mark: No, no, no. There is also the light of the six Bardos, we spoke about – the Gods, the Asuras, the humans, the Pretas, Hell and animal. (See diagram page 108.)

Question: That's another light?

Mark: Each one of those are different lights. Each one of those are worlds. But those don't appear until the Sidpa Bardo of the apparition of the new incarnation.

Question: Smoked color is bad, baby, right?

Mark: Black, smoky is hell, remember that; under no condition go into a black, smoky light. If you remember nothing else, remember that. (Laughter)

Question: I'm just wondering what effect drugs have on your encounter in the Bardo?

Mark: They affect the brain. They're manifesting in one of the six lobes of the brain and so they're conditioning it very intensely. It's better if a person who is dying from an intense disease where they're having intense pain and using pain management, drugs, to pull off of those drugs in the final moments because they will affect the brain and diminish the performance of the brain. If the pain is so much so that it is producing an anxiety as they approach death, it's a trade off. You're dealing with keeping the pain management drug in place to allow them to at least be physically comfortable while they are preparing mentally. You have to understand that you are affecting the brain's chemistry. If you're dealing with a loved one, if possible talk to them about it. In the final days have the drugs withdrawn. The brain will be clear. But it depends on how they want to do it.

Question: I'm also wondering about someone that has been on a spiritual path and is dying. Does it assist that person to have a fellow sangha member present?

Mark: It calms the mind. The power of the

relationship will produce an equilibrium. The best person to have present at the moment of death is your Guru. If you cannot have your actual Guru present, an agency of that Guru, like a fellow sangha member, will increase the power of the connection to the Guru. The person that's the fellow sangha member would meditate on the Guru as well so the presence of the Guru would be very strong in the room and also in the inner spiritual space as this occurred. You learn to call the Guru from afar within yourself and have the presence of the Guru in the room. Because the Guru is connected to the Great Light, the Guru can be present internally but without being present physically and they'll be waiting in the Bardo for you as you cross over and produce a beneficial impact on the unfoldment of the Bardo. This is actually one of the great reasons to have a Guru.

Question: I seem to remember from the Tibetan Book of the Dead that when someone goes into the Bardo, you're not supposed to touch them.

Mark: Don't touch them. You're right. Just sit quietly within yourself.

Question: My Irish Catholic birth family has very strong practices surrounding funerals and wakes and things like that and I find it unlikely that relatives would give me permission to hold their bodies for three days prior to going through those rituals.

Mark: Being moved just produces stress on the traveler. The attachment to the body is still present and when they wake up after the third day and they find their body in a morgue or if they were buried right away, they'll see that the body has been disposed of. What's most important is that you know what it's going to be. You should talk to your friends and family around you and say, "When I die, leave me alone for seven days and then burn my body", or whatever it is you want done.

If a person is connected to a religious system that has a specific custom, whatever they expect is what it should exactly be. If they expect to be taken to a wake of some kind and then there is going to be a service and then a funeral in X amount of days, as long as it's what it's supposed to be, they won't panic or be upset. They'll still be upset because there is always a subtle attempt to re-enter the body and they can't do it and that produces a kind of mounting tension until the process unfolds. So, absent the ability to control the body for three days, you should make sure that the people who are going to be in charge of taking care of your body know what you want done, and it should happen exactly that way. Then as it does happen you will feel all right about it.

Question: My question in regard to my family members is: If I could exert some control, what window of time would be helpful? 12 hours, 24 hours?

Mark: 24 hours would be helpful. Three days is best. Basically everything happens in three days, seven if you can.

Question: I've read that some Bodhisattvas intentionally incarnate in hell realms for purposes of their sadhanas?

Mark: Absolutely. You're dealing with an awakened reincarnation, an awakened rebirth, and they select what world system, what Bardo system they choose to incarnate in and they go through that gate.

Question: So they would choose that Dark Light and walk through it?

Mark: Yes, each Bardo sign has a signifier, an element, and basically all you have to do is give rise to that sign, to that alphabet, and the enlightened sangha will descend and there you'll be.

Question: There's a reverence and at the same time, a sense of humor in the way you describe it.

Mark: That's good. It's a serious subject. You've got to kind of keep it light. (Laughter)

Question: Don't bodies start to smell after a couple of days? What do you do about that?

Mark: Incense. (Laughter)

Question: Would you try to refrigerate the room? Would you bring the temperature down or is that distracting to the traveler?

Mark: No. That would actually probably be a good idea.

Question: I had an acquaintance who dealt with people dying a lot at an old folks home and typically they would put dry ice under the sheets next to the body and they would keep the body for four days maybe and at least people could come in and say goodbye.

Mark: Yeah, and we have that tradition of a wake where the body is held in state and everyone can come, touch the body and say goodbye.

Question: But just for that they would bring in some dry ice and put it under the small of the back ("I think that's a great idea and a good tip", says Mark) and maybe something next to the body under the sheets and it does pretty much... ("Slow the decay", says Mark)

Mark: Yeah, that wouldn't impede the spiritual process. We're talking about Western offsetting factors now. If they're lying down, leave them lying down. If they're sitting up, leave them sitting up and just let it go. In the West we are more uncomfortable with the presence of death and an unusual set of customs have come up. Usually a wake was seven days. Last day, everyone would show up, have a big party, and go bury him. The natural wisdom always has a place.

Question: With someone who has been practicing can you actually get to the point where you can control time as you move into the Bardo?

Mark: Hmmmm. Interesting question. I would say, yes, if you were of the enlightened sangha; no, if you're not of the enlightened sangha.

Question: In your classic, conventional haunting, is the person's spirit or soul or identity or some aspect literally still remaining in between this realm and the next?

Mark: They have entered one of the Bardos called *Preta*, which is the Bardo of the Hungry Ghost where out of affliction, terrible karma, desire, and extreme confusion, they have refused to enter the light and they have selected the Bardo of the Hungry Ghost. This means that they walk around in the physical world as a spirit, an energy presence, a mental presence, but they have no senses or body. What is usually involved when a preta or a ghost contacts a living being is they want to access their nervous system and their sensory system because the only way you can access this world is through the envelope of the physical body. If you lose the physical body, you can't touch this world. It's a very painful existence. If a person has committed great sins, etc. they can be forced into the preta existence through a mishandling of the Bardo movement. They exited through the wrong gate and they walked into the preta world. Once you're in the preta world, it's very hard to escape because you exist as an electrical force of life, a mind energy, with a very subtle mental frequency of life force. Usually once a person has become a hungry ghost, they'll remain a ghost for a long time, centuries even, and only a Guru with the power of shaktipat or grace can come along and bump them out of the preta existence.

Question: So that accounts for why a person will see an apparition with the same form for centuries? They're picking up the residual trace from that form?

Mark: What's really interesting is that they are accessing your form sense. They have lost formation. They don't have the power of form. This is what possession or haunting essentially is. They are accessing your reflex of formation and your mind reflex and you're seeing them in your mind essence with your form principle.

Question: So you do not actually perceive them directly, you perceive your response to them?

Mark: You will sometimes see a light or a shimmer, with your physical eyes but when it takes on a distinct form, what has happened is they've tapped. It's not subtle at all. When a preta taps you, it's like being touched by a finger. All of sudden you're aware of a presence. It's kind of a parasitical thing. They're trying to access your form sense and gain access to the circuitry of your senses so they can touch the world. They want to use your sensory perceptions to have experiences. What's intense about being a preta is that usually the reason you become a preta is that you're so attached to sensory experiences that you refused to leave the world and then before you knew it, you became stuck in this world as a preta. But the problem with being a preta is that you don't have the senses and you don't have formation, so you can't experience anything, but you still have desire to experience everything. So ghosts tend to be in an extreme state of psychic pain. In cases where a preta has existed for a long period of time, maybe in a place of power, they can gain enough power to become demonic forces where they are so powerful that they can actually overwhelm the mind of a human being and take over their body. It's very unlikely that a ghost would ever have that much energy to do it, but certainly some of the other darker forces might.

Question: So they had the option of leaving, but it's a very limited option?

Mark: A human being probably would not have the spiritual power to liberate a preta. Oftentimes what you'll see in cemeteries, the mores in South America, Day of the Dead in Mexico – you go to the grave and make offerings, etc. – it's a form of mercy, of feeding those in suffering. It's recognition of a genuine spiritual condition. Cemeteries are always very haunted and always very interesting places.

Question: What about the whole business though of wishing someone well, or telling them to go into the Light, or trying to somehow influence them in a positive way. Is that negligible?

Mark: I'll say it again. Thought is everything in the Bardo. What you think is what is.

Question: I've noticed when an animal dies, it seems that there will be an element of awareness present in the body long after the breath stops. The spirit doesn't just 'boom' check out.

Mark: That's what I'm talking about – the three days where the spirit, the body and the mind are deconstructed but they are still in connection.

Question: So that holds true for an animal as well as a human?

Mark: Yeah. To a lesser degree because there's a

less complex consciousness there but certainly to a degree.

Question: So it's a pretty miserable thing to just throw your pet in the ground and bury them right away?

Mark: If you have a pet and you love the pet, you definitely handle their process of transition as smoothly as you can.

Question: This thing that the soul comes out of the body at death, that's the way it is in the movies…?

Mark: It doesn't go out, it goes in. Death is not a door that closes, it opens.

Question: So you don't get to fly around your high school and see all your old buddies?

Mark: Unless you become a preta. But you will see everything in your mind. Everybody that's thinking of you at the moment of your death, you will see them as if they're right there. All time and space does dissolve. Everybody who is standing in the room, you will see into their deepest heart.

Question: My wife and I were with her grandfather

as he was dying and he said he was seeing his old relatives in the room with him, they came to see him. So everyone says that you have relatives that come to see you and they take you up to wherever you're going. Is that just something that is happening in your mind or are they actually taking you? Is that what is happening?

Mark: It would depend on the karmic connection. Like I said, the best person to have as a companion to death is your Guru. Second best is an agency of the Guru. Third best is someone who likes you or loves you like a family member.

Question: Are they (family members) really showing up and taking the dead to the Bardo or is that just an imagining?

Mark: It would be a thought-body. That's the thing – when we break out into the Bardo we go from desire-body to thought-body in the various stages of the Bardo.

Question: What about Alzheimers?

Mark: I've thought about that. That's tough because quite literally the pathways to the brain are breaking down. ("It runs in my family", says someone)

That's a tough one. Everything still works, but the person is lost in a dream anyway so it's hard for them to focus and it will be harder for them. That's why it's best if that person can at least fasten on to a point or a personality and gain the grace of a Guru. Lots of time people have friends and family that die and they let me know that they're dying. They're regular people. They may have some spiritual training of some kind or some religious attention, but not so much – they can still be worked with. Meditation helps and again, more than anything, it's connections. Having a connection to a force of relief can override almost any condition. I would say in a situation like Alzheimers a mantra would help focus a person. Any kind of name that is connected with God can be the mantra. When we enter into the Bardo we're dealing with thought-body forms of consciousness so anything that focuses the attention appropriately is desired.

Question: Is the triangular space the seat of the Guru? It feels like there is a space up there and there is kind of like a key that clicks in there.

Mark: Exactly so. There is a break in the sushumna between the seat of the Guru and about ¼ inch just on the other side of the outside of the skull. Learning to access that link of the sushumna is everything.

That point is the opening into the Great Light. When the Gurus give shaktipat, what happens is they switch that piece of the brain on and then the Guru is always present as a form of awakening. It's like the single drop of curd into a barrel of milk. That single drop will transform that entire barrel of milk into yogurt. A single touch of awakening at the seat of the Guru will turn the entire mind-body-heart matrix into the Clear Light.

Question: So is that what happens in Samadhi before you die?

Mark: Yes, that light opens, it locks in and it starts to pour in just like it was the Great Light at the moment of death but you're holding on to the body so the body becomes a part of what is remaindered. For most people when they start to go into Samadhi, the light overwhelms the connection to the body, even after a few days. There are a couple of yogic tricks to hang on to the body. Oftentimes you'll see if a person starts to go into Samadhi, the body will last for maybe another year or so and then they'll merge. Some will merge at the moment of Samadhi.

This lineage is a Siddha lineage. The word "Siddha" is interesting; it's very educating. To be a Siddha, we don't have a doctrine or a system of belief that one represents something else. The Siddha path is one where you yourself are transformed and become the thing. In other words, the light comes in and it transforms you into that thing. You're not separate from it. It's not an idea or a form. You experience it directly as yourself. Siddhas are specific kinds of beings and the transmission is of a certain kind. This is the Siddha lineage so the pathway tends to go along the lines of awakening and transformation inside the mind-body. The tendency of this lineage at this time is that people who are gaining enlightenment are keeping the body. I think it's best because it's the nature of the time. If everybody merged at the moment they hit Samadhi, then there would be nobody to grind it out in the earth plane.

Question: What happens in the Tibetan tradition with the rainbow body?

Mark: Well, that's interesting. The rainbow body is very rare and it represents an extremely exalted enlightenment where all of the constituents of ones' being are transformed into light. As the Great Light goes into the sushumna, ida and pingala, the six chakras, the five elements and the 100 fibers, it even grabs the physical body and transforms it into light. So nothing is left when you die but the fingernails, the hair and the teeth. It's cool.

Question: Isn't this talk supposed to be given at the morgue or something like that? In the old days the Guru would take you down to where all the dead bodies where.

Mark: It's classic that it's held in cemeteries.

Question: Don't they meditate in the place where the dead are?

Mark: Yes. It's like a Chöd in that way.

Question: Is it possible to choose the moment of death?

Mark: Tulku can choose the moment of death, choose the moment of life and choose the quality of the incarnation at the arising of thought itself. (editor's note: A tulku is a Tibetan Buddhist lama who, through phowa and siddha, has consciously determined to be reborn, often many times, in order to continue their Bodhisattva vow.)

I'm operating on this side; I'll be operating on that side. It's the same.

Question: What about abortion?

Mark: Well, it would be a form of negation. It's a very dicey subject. There you are in the womb gate and all of a sudden you're gone.

Question: Do you go through the Bardo again?

Mark: Yup! Well you would be alive and then you'd have to face death again. So it does give one pause, but life is tough. One more lap around the track.

Question: Shouldn't that second time really be a little easier, a little clearer?

Mark: Yeah, you wouldn't have built much karma up, so in that way, it could probably work in your favor.

Question: What is the Judgment day? We have this Judeo-Christian concept of what that means. What does it mean to you?

Mark: All of the karma, every single intention of every single action in this incarnation releases out of the 58 wrathful deities. They are along the spine and they flood into the brain. The brain experiences the content of every white karma and every black karma and reduces them to an algorithm in the brain/mind matrix. The mind is a mirror. It has no substance of its own. It reflects what it comes into contact with, so every single thought is reduced to a single byte of data. If you accept the Judgment, then you live out the Judgment in the next seven days with the onslaught of the 58 wrathful deities.

Question: Well that's the part I don't understand. Does that mean that it's possible to receive a judgment that precludes you from going through the wrathful procession?

Mark: Yeah.

Question: So it isn't necessary for every individual to go through the wrathful stage?

Mark: You can leave at any point. The first day of the wrathful procession is the manifestation of God as the Guru. If you recognize God as the Guru, all of your sins are wiped away and you gain liberation right then and there and the wrathful procession does not occur.

Question: But I'm trying to understand the Judgment. Can the Judgment be such that the Judgment says it's not necessary for you to go through the next fourteen days of hell?

Mark: There's always the aspect of performance in the Bardo. It is possible to NOT accept the Judgment. You should not accept it – you should see it as the Clear Light of Reality.

Question: What is the Judgment? You keep saying "don't accept it". I think of the Judgment as being you're good or you're bad, what does that mean?

Mark: Good and evil are religious concepts. They have no reality. The Judgment is a mirror, the mirror of your existence. It's held up to you.

Question: This seems incomprehensible to me. It seems to me from what you said, that a human being is in essence being punished by the wrathful deities because of the "I" ego understanding. If you have the "I" ego, then you must go through the wrathful deities. If you don't then you don't have to go through that.

Mark: If you're still stuck in the Bardo it is because you still have the "I" ego. You're not being punished. You'll experience it as punishment because of your attachment to "I". All that's happening is that consciousness is becoming aggressive and attacking the ignorance of your false refuge. But you're stuck on it. Let me say it again…the Judgment is the mirror of your existence. Every karma of your existence is held up to you as a mirror. The mirror is your mind. If you believe in an "I" – "Yes, I did all of those things" – then that is the acceptance of your Judgment. On the other hand, if you say the mind is void and empty by nature, having no quality, there's nothing there to be judged and it doesn't happen.

Question: If you really take the whole concept contextually, it seems incredibly flawed and biased. A human being is born and there's nobody in this arena telling us that we are not an "I" ego being, that we are a part of universal consciousness. So in essence, we go through this whole realm of humanity – unless you're graced to find a Guru to open you up and awaken you – you're basically stuck in this place where everyone is asleep and then you die and go into the Bardo and every construct that you have ever created in your human life of what a horror show is, what hell is, you're faced to confront fifteen days of that because you believe exactly what you were told to believe by your life.

Mark: That's exactly true.

Question: When you think of a higher intelligence creating this system, it's punishing someone for thinking what the higher intelligence told you to think. The higher intelligence is God who created us.

Mark: The concept of a second thing is not so. You and God are both the Clear Light of Reality. I'm functioning as the Guru.

Question: You're here to tell us that, but you're one of twelve on the planet. Every other person out there says that's nonsense.

Mark: I know. It is a problem. I'm not saying it isn't. (Laughter)

Question: Even though the system seems so weird, there seems to be all these opportunities to hop off.

Mark: Yeah, look at the glass half full.

Question: If you've got a Guru, you're set. If you've got a Guru, you've got a wild card. To me the whole deck seems incredibly rigged. If you have a Guru you should be able to escape this whole process. There's a million ways to get out.

Mark: Following your logic, if the system is so rigged against us, we have to give as many opportunities to get out as possible.

Question: It's only a few people who get dealt the wild card. Everybody else doesn't. And the bizarre element of the Bardo, which is really the part that blows my mind, is that 99.9% of the people who enter the Bardo don't want enlightenment anyway. They want to come back here. So the whole thing that is being perpetrated is kind of like torturing them for wanting to come back here. Even if you said to them, you could go to enlightenment or whatever…

Mark: They couldn't conceive of enlightenment, that's right.

Question: That's what the whole Bardo is about, giving up personal desire. They don't want to give up personal desire, right?

Mark: It's a machine of creation. It's an engine.

Question: It's like a high blood pressure test. You wrap it around your arm, you pump it up and it tells you how much desire you have. Up to a certain level and you're thrown back into the pile and you start all over again.

Mark: We've talked about this before because we're in the first quarter of the last stage of this cycle of the Creation, the Kali Yuga. We've gone from a multi-thousand year incarnation to a seventy year length incarnation. We've moved the life force out of the mass of the bone into the prana and we've got the entire enlightened sangha generating shaktipat on sight without the slightest preparation, still shoveling shit against the tide. But mass shaktipat is very powerful. Basically mass shaktipat is also mass phowa. Is there the likelihood that you're going to master phowa between now and your death? Yes and no, but the authority is given to make up for what inabilities you have to carry you past that into the enlightened condition simply by aligning with the Guru.

I can see where the sages have looked at the system and said, well this is the system; it's like an engine. They've basically said that God created the engine of the creation and not even God will change his own creation. But the Guru has the ability to manifest mercy because the Guru was invented as the grace bestowing power of God. It's the incarnation of mercy so the Guru is flowing through the system trying to find any point where the situation can be turned positive from an almost hopeless game. Without the Guru there would be no chance and that is even grimmer.

Question: The one element which I thought you left out is what the effect is of shaktipat in the Bardo.

Mark: I was using the phowa on that. Shaktipat in the Bardo gives you almost an automatic perfect phowa. You'll be able to transfer your consciousness directly from your body into the Clear Light of Reality by having shaktipat. I thought that I implied that.

I've given shaktipat to countless people that have never met me personally. And they will be able to do phowa. The more meditation, the more dharma, the more practice, the better for them. It will increase their performance capacity and their endurance capacity in a highly stressful situation. Once you get shaktipat you go on the list of the lineage. You're marked; you're tagged. When your condition comes up, a beeper goes off and grace occurs. It's very profound.

Question: So, is that you? Is it the individual who imparts the grace of shaktipat who is connected to that individual when they pass through the Bardo?

Mark: The Guru that is incarnate at the end of a lineage is like a lightening rod that carries the totality of the whole. It's not my personal power that is doing it. It is the lineage and the energy of the shaktipat that is connected to my consciousness.

Question: But shaktipat is sufficient to take a person to Siddhaloka or to the higher worlds?

Mark: Yes. They will be drawn upward inexorably. There is a tag that you can achieve enlightenment in a single lifetime or up to sixteen lifetimes. Once you receive shaktipat and even if you never do anything after that, in sixteen lifetimes you would be completely liberated.

Question: In all the time I've been studying with you, I've never gotten that message.

Mark: That's why I don't say it. Because that would be what everybody would hear. (Laughter) Because people are really funny.

Question: I'm still thinking about the triangle. Why wouldn't we want to do that right now? Is that what we are doing right now?

Mark: Yes, you could do that every day between now and the rest of your incarnation and chances are you will merge with the Great Light of Reality before death.

Question: Does that mean visualizing yourself going out?

Mark: You start with visualization and you hone in. Things just are what they are. There's no second thing. Once you understand, you just recognize the truth of it and it occurs.

Question: You're talking in such ambiguous-crazy-profound terms that I can't even fathom what you're saying, and you keep saying, "No, no, it's not visual, it's just feeling it", but for me all I can do is visualize it.

Mark: So go with visual. You go with where you are and that's your handle and that will advance. If you seat the Guru on the crown of your head you will merge your personal individuality with the Dharmakaya.

Question: Is that visualizing you sitting on my head?

Mark: Whatever works for you. Any kind of sign of the Guru. I personally used the form of the Guru and the form of the Guru's feet. It's great.

Question: I've never seen your feet. (Laughter)

Mark: Two favorite tennis shoes. (Laughter) Why do you think that I have so many shoes? There is a method to that madness. I'm trying to make an impression.

Question: How does Meher Baba fit into the Guru's......?

Mark: Meher Baba was the last physical manifestation of God. He will arise as God and Guru. He will do everything. The Guru is not a person, place or thing. The Guru is an eternal spirit that arises as God and however you want to signify the Guru, that's up to you. It's very personal, very direct. You can call on the whole lineage of Gurus.

This concludes our Kunda session on the Bardo Thodol. Om Swaha

Bardo Question & Answer Satsang
March 8, 2007

Last Saturday we had our first Kunda of the year. The subject was the Bardo of Life and Death and the interval of the intermediate state. We employed dual speech in that on the level of verbal cognition we had an unfolding explanation of the Bardo Thodol. At the same time along the line of internal spiritual speech, through the power of Samadhi, through the power of the supra conscious state, we actually traversed the interval of the intermediate state, which is the state of consciousness between life and death.

This process of spiritual transformation is the same for all human beings regardless of religion, culture, time or place. It simply will dress itself up in the language of the individual according to their understanding, their belief system, and their cultural impressions. It is thus very important to have a grasp of this very dynamic moment when the arrival of the interval occurs. When understood appropriately, it guarantees liberation upon contact.

Saturday was a very dramatic day and an enormous amount of information, both internal and external was expressed, so I wanted to dedicate this session to Satsang Q & A on the Bardo Thodol. Due to the depth and intensity of this teaching, it seems that some questions may have arisen.

Question: I remember that you've mentioned that there's an opportunity for you to say who your teacher was in the Bardo. When does that happen? It seemed like it was about three steps down from the first opportunity.

Mark: What you're referring to happens in The Judgment, however the Guru appears between each of the stages of the Bardo, and at any point that you recognize the Guru you will become liberated and enlightened.

The first opportunity is the moment the symptoms of death begin to occur and the prana begins to fold in from the extremities, the heat begins to escape from the body, escape from the core, senses begin to dim, the body begins to turn to stone, the mind starts to collapse and begins to fade and the senses switch off. The collapse of the elements from earth into water, water into fire, fire into air, air into ether, each of which are accompanied by very loud, disconcerting and disorienting phenomenon because the senses are supported by the elements. As the senses collapse inside the architecture of the life force, one feels that one is in earthquakes, floods – there is kind of a conflagration quality as the life force and the structure of identity collapses. At this point the breath begins to fade. There will be a moment as the breath fades, where the breath will simply stop between an in-breath and an out-breath or between an out-breath and an in-breath. At that moment the Clear Light will dawn spontaneously, the very second the breath stops. That is the first opportunity to give rise to the consciousness of the Guru. Draw the Guru to the crown of the head and at the very moment that the Clear Light dawns, merge with the Guru. You'll be absorbed into the Guru because the Guru is of the nature of the Clear Light. You'll be drawn into the Clear Light and you'll be enlightened and liberated at the very moment.

After that, you'll go through a phase of events. If you do merge with the Clear Light, it's called the moment of consciousness transference. If you don't merge, there will be an unfolding set of conditions, each as if you were going down a step. Having failed to recognize the Clear Light, you'll go into a three-day trance. During that three days you will live in the intermediate state; you will exist between life and death during which time you will see your entire life, you will see and hear the hearts and minds of all of the people around you, all the people that are in your life, whether they are near you or far. At that moment of time when space collapses there is a very intense darshan of your existence. You will see your dead body. You will try to re-enter it and you won't be able to enter it. This will go on for three days – a kind of progressive realization that one has actually died. It can last anywhere as long as it takes for a meal to be eaten, it could last as long as the snapping of one's fingers, or it can last up to three days. If one merges with the Great Light, one can actually sit inside the body in the intermediate state, merged with the Great Light for anywhere up to three to seven days. In some conditions of very profound masters, they stay in their bodies for eternity. The condition is not as if you are living inside of a rotting corpse because your consciousness has merged with the Great Light, so you are one with the Great Light, but there is the intention of the yogi to maintain a contact with his enlightened identity with that place in the body and that place and that time on earth to provide a system for accessing the Great Light onto the plane of the earth.

This idea of progressing through the first Bardo is called the Chikhai Bardo and that is the first appearance of the Great Light and the three-day dream whereupon you see your body and try to re-enter it. This is why the general wisdom is that when a person dies, you leave their body alone. You don't touch it for three days. You're allowing the person to go through the full cycle of their process. It's kind of like a dream, like a stupor, a deep hallucination, but you are mentally experiencing all of the dynamics of your life. Then there is a point where you will emerge from that dream and the Great Light will appear again. Often times this is where people are willing to release. The very first second of the death of the body there is still karmic attachment by the mind to the body and you still haven't said your goodbyes. There is a very strong tendency to hold on for a few days. But usually after three days you come to understand that you have died and you have no access to the body. You can straighten out your thinking – "I am now in the intermediate state and it's time for me to move on." At which time, again give rise to the Guru.

Remember we were talking about the form of the Bodhicitta at the crown of the head, the White Bodhicitta, coming to the heart, the Red Bodhicitta at the navel rising to the heart. The Bodhicitta is of the form of the Great Light – the polar opposition of the

Great Light upon which the Creation rests. When you bring them into the heart they will transform into the Guru. At that point if you simply call the Guru, the Guru will arise and manifest at the crown of the head – where it will flood the brain, flood the mind, flood the sushumna, capture the seat of the Bodhicitta and carry the soul out through the crown of the head. The soul is liberated and enlightened at that point.

If that fails, there is the beginning of the onset of karmic conditions. At each point of the onset of karmic conditions, it is possible to remember the Guru. The Guru will always appear when the Bardo moves from one stage to another. You will see the Guru somewhere in the Bardo. After a while it begins to take on a kind of hallucination; this wild dream will begin forming just like this life. It will be made up of the thought-constructs of your own mind, thought-constructs of your own heart and mixed up in those thought-constructs you will see the Guru. Like in the dream, you're walking down a road and you walk up to a house, and you walk into the house and sitting in a chair in the house is the Guru. If you recognize him as the Guru, the Great Light will form, you'll be drawn out of the Bardo and you'll be liberated and enlightened.

There is a formal moment, the moment of the

Judgment, in the middle of the Chonyid Bardo, after you've gone through all of the first stages of the unfoldment of the karmic conditions that take place in the 42 peaceful deities. They are part of the strands of the fibers of the sushumna that emerge out of the chakras. The peaceful deities arise out of the heart center; the wrathful deities arise out of the brain center. In this place between the two, there is a condition called The Judgment. What happens there is that the entire karmic load of the identity dumps into the central nerve and produces the event of The Judgment. It's characterized as the scales of white and black stones. The white stones represent good karma; the black stones represent bad karma. It's also propelled by the astrological equation that moves in the subtle nerves that generate the pranic winds. All of these are producing the Bardo, as you are in the interval of the intermediate state.

The intermediate state is exactly like this world. It's almost impossible to tell the difference. Once it starts, your mind will invent one dream after another that will be perfectly sewn together to produce a reality that exactly expresses the karmic content of your own thought-constructs – your friends, your family, all of your desires and all of your conditions will appear in your dream as your dream.

The Judgment is a movement that is halfway between

the interval of the peaceful and wrathful deities, where all of the karma dumps into the sushumna and pours into the brain. The equilibrium of the brain is where the seeds of the astrological equation of your identity lie. It's the clock. At that point the dream will take on a kind of interrogation. What was the meaning of your life? And you have an opportunity to say something and it plays out as a form of thought. At that moment if you remember to say that you got shaktipat from such and such a Guru at such and such a time, it's like having a powerful friend that gets you out of jail and The Judgment will fade and you'll be liberated and enlightened at that moment.

Even after, if you go through the entire Judgment in a condition of confusion and the unfoldment of positive and negative karmas progress and you have still forgotten to recognize the Great Light and forgotten to give rise to the Guru, the Guru will spontaneously appear right after The Judgment. If you recognize the Guru, you're liberated and enlightened. If you fail to recognize the Guru, then the onslaught of the wrathful deities occurs.

At that point things get more and more difficult because the word 'wrathful' means that the dream of the Bardo becomes frightening. Up until then it will tend to reflect your life. You'll see your friends, your family, your loved ones, your car, your dog and your cat. You'll be driving down the road in the car and you'll drive to a house and there will be somebody that you know, or all of a sudden you'll be riding in the car and you look over and it's the Guru driving the car. You'll be having those kinds of dreams. Once it becomes wrathful, it becomes frightening. The wrathful deities tend to take on fearful imagery – blood drinking demons, etc. It's the whole thing in folk wisdom that everyone speaks of – angels and demons that carry you to the next world. They are in fact your own thought-constructs unfolding as you move inside the interval of the intermediate state between life and death.

If at any point you give the time, place and person that you got shaktipat from, that will bring the full force of the Guru and the full force of the lineage to bear on your situation and they will just wrap you up and pull you out and save you. That's why it's important to get used to the presence of the Guru so that at the point where you're under the condition of intense psychological stress of the death process, you can bring the grace and power of the Guru to heart and mind and use that as a doorway to transfer your consciousness into the Great Light. It's everything. This transference of consciousness thing is great and anybody can do it. You just have to have the peace of mind to do it.

There are two things in the balance. There is free will. You have to allow a person to meet the unfoldment of his or her conditions. It's like you're being fed information, making it easier and the best condition is always sought. It's one of the most important moments in your relationship with the Guru. A lot of what's happening as we go through all of these meditations is that I'm showing you the real world, the inner world and there's a part of you that's recording it. So when the moment of truth comes, it won't seem that foreign. It won't even seem that scary. It's kind of like it's sort of scary, but it's not that scary.

Question: If so much rests on remembering to call on the Guru, does it make sense to do it 20 times a day, just so that you're constantly thinking about the Guru? So that if you end up dying and you don't notice and you're in a dream you would call on the Guru out of habit?

Mark: Yeah, that is wisdom. You want to have that as a reflex so that your connection to the Guru is so complete, so fulfilled, that there is no gap. It's one of the reasons why Hard Light and Baba employ the activation of the SoHam. The manifestation of awakening between God, Guru and Self takes place at the SoHam. Every time you breathe you say the mantra that is the awakening vehicle because there's a moment at death where breath stops, just like in samadhi. When you go into samadhi the interval between the positive and negative breath has ceased and you are in the empty interval between breaths. Also OM NAMAH SHIVAYA. The mantra is God is the Guru is the Self. It's a very powerful device just as a straight vibrational pneumonic device. In any condition you just say OM NAMAH SHIVAYA – that's it, "whoooooosh", consciousness transference, it's over.

Question: Do you want to be saying the mantra as you're dying?

Mark: Yeah, it can't hurt. The thing about the Bardo is that it is sudden. As it moves, all of the things that are going on are very swift and sudden. It's a quality of experience that you've not had before so there is a shock dynamic and one of the reactions of shock is forgetfulness, like how you forget your name in an intense state of shock, and so you want to have those devices very close at hand to offset the shock value. On the other side, if you stay calm with it, it's extremely dramatic and the dice are really rolling.

Quite literally, enlightenment is a fruit in your hand if you simply call the Guru and transfer consciousness into the Great Light. It is the moment where most people achieve liberation because they'll do sadhana for their whole life, they'll hang out and gain power, generate and deepen their relationship to the Guru, live out the lifetime until the separation of the mind from the body and death arises. If you handle that moment right, you become enlightened. It's rare that a person transfers their consciousness into the Great Light while holding on to the body. And even if they hold on to the body, the intensity of transferring their consciousness into the Great Light is so dramatic that you actually have to produce a set of countervailing yogic practices to continually hang onto the body. At the moment of death all of those issues are moot and you can merge directly, transfer your consciousness directly into the Great Light through the gateway of the Guru. It is practically failsafe. If you are in a situation where death is known to be approaching, a message should be sent to the Guru so the Guru knows in real time that it is happening and their attention is drawn to your condition.

One of the things that you'll notice when a person does make the movement of transference of consciousness is that there will tend to be a sign after it's completed. If the consciousness principle goes out the eyes, the eyes will become very bloodshot. If the consciousness goes out the crown of the head, there might be just a small little pinprick open where a little drop of blood will appear. Sometimes advanced yogis will sit in the state between life and death, in the intermediate state, for days, weeks, months or years. It's always recorded that a yellow liquid comes out of all of their orifices after a certain point as the tissues come into the intense spiritual fire of the Great Light. Everything is kind of mummified, cooked down.

Question: You say "Merge with the Great Light." What does that actually entail? What does that mean? Does that mean bring it into your heart?

Mark: It rolls into you first as though the ocean were pouring into you. It comes in and it flies down the sushumna, flies down the ida and pingala and you're immediately reduced to that light. If you are an advanced yogi you will reduce yourself to the White and Red Bodhicitta. Because of the quality of advanced yogis, the process of their death is filled with mystery and spiritual intention. If they choose to elongate the event, they'll sit in the condition of Nirvikalpa Samadhi, in nirvana and they're not leaving the body. The White Bodhicitta will drop to the heart; the Red Bodhicitta will rise to the heart and it will hold there. You'll feel an incredible blast of energy coming out of this shell – it's a corpse now but based on their mastery of time and space, they can stay in that condition for however long they want.

We were talking about Nityananda. When you go to Nityananda's temple, he's down there and he's in the state of the Nirvikalpa, the punyatithi, the merging of the Great Light in his tomb and you are aware of that because there is just an ocean of light pouring out of his sarcophagus. It's not at all distant. It's very, very intense, very active. Muktananda did the same thing. He's buried deeper into the ground, but he's buried in a meditative state. Other times a person will sit for three, five, ten days, then they'll be complete and the body is to be burned. As the consciousness pervades with the body, there are a series of relics where pieces of the skull will crystallize because they're so saturated with the Great Light that in the intense heat of the fire they turn into pieces of crystals. Those become relics that are held in the various temples.

If you fail to recognize the movement of the Great Light you will be knocked into a kind of hallucination and this is where you will see the unfoldment of your life in a kind of dreamlike state, including the place where your body is. You'll sense that you're in the intermediate state, the after death state, and your body is in the creation of the world and you won't be able to get to it.

With a person it's not necessary to hang on to the body for very long. They say that the average person will hold a spiritual state of the onslaught of the Great Light for the length of a meal. The amount of time it takes to eat a meal, you will be in the intermediate state and merge with the Great Light. At that point you will merge out and your consciousness principle will be absorbed as if a drop of your individual consciousness merges with the ocean and you will exit out the crown of the head and you will be enlightened and liberated. If you wait through the whole dream it will take anywhere from the snapping of the fingers, the length of a meal, to three days. The next appearance of the Great Light you have the same opportunity to merge with it.

Question: In terms of understanding this merging with the Great Light, when a layman confronts this light, is it like standing there and seeing the light of a ten billion suns in front of you?

Mark: For an instant you'll see that, kind of like seeing a nuclear blast of a million suns going off and then it overwhelms you.

Question: Then it overwhelms everyone who is in the Bardo?

Mark: Yeah. When you merge with it, you no longer see it. You're just part of it.

Question: But you said that generally the average person doesn't merge with it and that's why the Bardo continues on. Correct?

Mark: Right. With all of that power, it is possible that if you generate the reflex of fear and rejection you will maintain a kind of solidity. Even though you're suspended in the Great Light, you will not merge with it. You're merged with the Great Light now but you don't know it and so that unconsciousness continues. There's a part of you that kind of cracks open when you merge. The Great Light and the Creation merge into each other and they crack open and just fill each other. It's a very blissful sensation.

Question: Is it a conditioned response?

Mark: Yes, the conditioned response is rejection because the reflex of attachment to the body has connected to it an extension of protection to the body. If you are attached to the body you will experience the onslaught of the Great Light as a threat to the body.

Question: So generally all of us will feel threatened by our initial meeting with the Great Light?

Mark: That's why if you have the opportunity to prepare for death, do it. Death is coming and you can feel it. Death is not subtle. When it's around, it's really clear that it's around. Your body starts to go through all the reflexes and you go, "Oh my God, I'm dying." That's why I say, sit up, keep your spine straight, begin to prepare yourself. Call on the Guru, call on God, arouse your courage and know that as you go through the collapse that this is the process of the separation of the mind from the body. The first thing you're going to see is the light of a billion suns and know that that is God. You're just going to dive into it when you see it. You resolve to do it. It's like jumping off a cliff. You stand there and you're afraid to jump and then some part of you overrides and you just do it – like jumping out of an airplane.

Question: It isn't necessary then to manipulate the Red and White Bodhicitta in order to merge with the Great Light?

Mark: That would be an advanced condition if you were capable of doing that. That way you could sit in a merged condition for an extended amount of time, which expresses a deeper expression of enlightenment. The ability to do that is a sign of mastery.

Question: OK, but for the rest of us, if we could just manage to move towards it and jump into it that would be great. ("Right", says Mark) Even though that's contrary to the laws of being attracted or repelled to something, I thought that the whole concept of enlightenment is to be neither attracted nor repelled.

Mark: Well, like they say, enlightenment is the nonattractive attraction. If you're going to be attracted to anything, be attracted to God.

Question: I think you define this trip as 49 days, right?

Mark: If you go through every stage of the Bardo from the separation of the mind from the body all the way to the rebirth process and entry into a new womb, it's a 49 days cycle.

Question: Does every person who dies go through 49 days other than those who merge with the Great Light, or can your karma necessitate a shorter visitation with the wrathful deities for example?

Mark: Absolutely everything is conditioned by karma, ability, karmic conditions and connections.

Question: We're getting to the big question. There

are two things that you said that really shook me up that I'm trying to understand. The first one which is always this prevalent concept of spirituality, is that there is no good or bad, and you said something like the visitation in the Bardo has nothing to do with whether you were good or bad. Is that true?

Mark: Absolutely. Everything that happens in the Bardo is the animation of your own thought-constructs. It is you.

Question: When you say that the fibers in the body are in essence the memories of all thoughts and actions, are we being judged on all those thoughts and actions?

Mark: The weight and balance of those thoughts and actions produce a perfect algorithm that conditions the next birth.

Question: Well there has to be a criterion for evaluating those fibers.

Mark: Yes, it's the criterion of life.

Question: Which is what? Isn't that good and bad?

Mark: No, life is just a magnetic field that holds qualities together. Death is a field that causes them to part.

Question: What I'm really talking about is understanding the most frightening part of death for all mankind. All the way down through the ages there is this perception of the devil, the heat, hell and all the rest of it. It's the negative that frightens people. It isn't the positive. We have heaven on the positive side. So I'm trying to understand in terms of the wrathful deities, what's going on, and if that can be curtailed and how the average individual's meeting with the wrathful deities goes. I gather from everything I've read that it's pretty damn horrific. It seems to be from what you've said that the purpose of the wrathful deities is to shock the individual. Because the individual's consciousness is wrapped up in the I-ego separation between the individual and God, and the individual is not capable of perceiving that they and the infinite are one, and because of that failure to understand and comprehend universal consciousness the wrathful deities are there to shock the hell out of the individual until they merge with the Clear Light. Is that correct?

Mark: Well, it's better to think of it as cause and effect, without that intentional shock element; it's more of a universal principle. For every cause, an effect arises. They're not two things. They arise simultaneously. They may seem to be delayed in time, but that is a misapprehension of perception. The cause and the effect arise simultaneously as one thing. It is a misapprehension that there is any time between the two. The wrathful deities are the messengers of the effect of your cause. They're not separate from you; they are you. They are your own mind manifesting in karmically conditioned forms. In other words, if the mind operated in a series of actions that expressed the poisons of greed, anger, hatred, etc. those thought-constructs would be present in the mind and they would manifest as part of the formation of the wrathful deities. But it's just an apparition; it's just a dream. Just like last night you dreamt of a tiger. Was there a tiger? And the tiger ate you in the dream and you woke up in your bed this morning. Why did the tiger eat you? Were you the reward for the tiger's good karma and he found you and ate you and had food or was the tiger punishment for something you did, so the tiger found you and killed you and ate you? It's completely arbitrary. There's no *there* there. There's no objectiveness to any quality. So to try to produce an apprehension of any quality as good or evil is again completely arbitrary.

Question: Haven't you talked about greed, envy and lust being the negative qualities that one should avoid?

Mark: Well they're negative because they produce a kind of separation. The fabrics of the poisons are not bad in any inherent way, but they have a cohesion to them that doesn't break down. Just examine your own mind when you're in the throes of anger. Your mind is operating at a very low level of clarity and skill. It's operating irrationally. It's making irrational leaps. It's coming to false assumptions. The liver is pouring chemistry into the system that is toxifying the system and you produce a very intense condition of separation. It's an effect. The effect of anger is separation.

Question: When I spoke before about being punished by the wrathful deities for ego separation, those qualities that you're speaking of carry the charge of separation. That's what propels the whole play then.

The one thing you want to remember about the wrathful deities is that they are just your own thought-constructs. Whatever your own thought-constructs were, it's all stripped down to exactly what it was. Even if it happened before, it's stored in the system. That's why they call it The Judgment. Everything that happens from the beginning of this life to the end of this life is dumped and happens all at once. That's why it's wrathful. The word wrathful means sudden, like a jove. A jove is a wrathful angel.

Mark: That's what propels the play. And it's just what it is. That's why I say it's the perfect algorithm. To the extent that you produce the seeds of anger, let's say 20,000 times in the course of a lifetime, those seeds will produce the effect of separation and the effect of separation will take the form of the wrathful deities.

Question: Paramahamsa Yogananda's body was viewed in state for months at a time. He was put in a glass-enclosed case. The concept was to show people that his body didn't decay. I'm not sure how many months it was, but it was a heck of a show and it made a big effect on western minds here. Would that indicate that he didn't leave the body?

Mark: Yes, during that time he would be in a condition of nirvana.

Question: After Saturday I concluded that this whole process is 'the joke's on you'. I was wondering if I'm going through this whole process as a form of recognition and the joke's on me, if I just laugh at myself, would that be a form of recognition?

Mark: Absolutely. It's actually one of the things that is notable for the moment of recognition is that it is always a really bad joke. It has been right in front of your face all this time and you've just kept getting it wrong. And all of a sudden you go "Oh, it's so simple."

Question: So it's really funny actually. You're saying that there is nothing different from this side to the other side. It's all an illusion?

Mark: Life and death are the same. In the dream of life, it plays out in the illusion of time. In the intermediate state, time ceases to operate in quite the same way. Everything arises at once.

Question: If I don't take it seriously, I think that takes away the seriousness of that.

Mark: Yeah and one of the ways to think about not taking it seriously is if you have the karma of existence, there is an intention to your existence. It is native to existence itself. So you'll find that some people are compelled to do different kinds of things. Some people are compelled by their karma to be a soldier. Some people are compelled by their karma to be a healer, etc. – you're just drawn to it. It's an unfoldment of your fate, of your destiny. To not take it seriously is (1) to do everything the best you can and (2) do not seek the fruit of the action. Just give it everything. All action is given as service to God and there's no sense of "Oh, if I do this, I'm going to get this." As soon as you start doing that, then the poisons start to creep in and then you're thinking in terms of greed. But if you are alert at the moment of the action itself, as you do it while you do it, you'll find that the entire cause and effect arises at the same time.

This thing about desire – 'If I do this, then I will get this' – is a complete illusion. Almost in no cases is a person who thinks that correct. And you often see that's true. Most people are doing things for reasons that have nothing to do with reality. And if you ever ask 'Why are you doing this?' and they tell you, and you were a fly on the wall and watched their lives, almost in no cases do the things they want come to them in quite the same way they thought they would. And this is where people will get confused and bitter. "What's the meaning of life, I didn't get anything that I wanted." And it turns out that you got everything you had coming to you and more.

But there's a kind of freedom of heart and spirit. I always liked Don Juan's term called "controlled falling." It's a very descriptive term that implied the highest skill, the highest intention, giving it everything you've got but the complete open hand in attachment to the results. It's a very advanced condition. It's called detachment in our lexicon, and detachment speaks of the difference between the soul and the karma of the body. The body has a karma all its own. You get your fingers caught in doorjambs and you got sick when you were twelve years old and this many things happened to you and that many things didn't happen to you and there's something involved and integrated, but there's a detachment there because the soul is in a different condition. The true identity is some place else. When you understand that, you can actually learn to cause your mind and your actions to be completely free. Everything that's going to come to you will come to you. It can't be stopped. On the other hand, everything that's going to come to you is going to come to you and you can't cause it to happen, it just happens.

The skill lies in aligning the mind, the heart, the body and the action with the truth of the Self. When you do that you live a completely fulfilled life. Whatever you did in your life was completely your karma. Whether you were a king, a soldier, whatever, it was completely yours and that gives meaning to life. What happened to you had meaning, it had content and you feel full. If you get off that track and it is just a product of imagination, it will carry no weight, it will have no fruit, it will have no rasa. That is the underlying spirit of, "Yes! Live life with joy."

Question: So essentially when the time comes, you're harvesting your own cosmology, whatever you've invested yourself in, whatever you've imagined is real or is not real, whatever you've used to construct your sense of what is going on, that's what you will experience when the time comes?

Mark: Yes, the collapsing of the five elements, the onslaught of the symptoms of death, the switching off of the senses, the detachment of the mind from the body, the Great Light and the unfoldment of karmic conditions, etc. – all of the elements will be driven by the mechanics of the intermediate state. Something is causing it to occur and that is the separation of the mind from the body, the bringing into equilibrium of karma, the opportunity for the transference of consciousness into the Great Light – and if that is missed, the cycling back into the birth cycle, rebirth and the achievement of a new womb and a new body. The imagery will be reflected by the content of your own thought but the underlying purpose will be the same for everyone. If you grew up in Japan and you were a Buddhist, the imagery will tend to have Buddhist overtones. If you don't particularly believe in one God or another, the Bardo will take on the form of your internal cosmology. It will take the universe of your thoughts and produce them as an unfolding Bardo.

Question: So you will be confronted by whatever you attribute to being outside of yourself. If you think that there are wonderful magic things outside of you, then you'll experience not being able to reach them. If you think there are terrible bad people in the world that behave in ways that deserve to be punished...

Mark: It cannot be stated strongly enough that the tambour of thought is everything in the Bardo – in the living condition of the Bardo, in the death condition of the Bardo and in the intermediate state. What you think immediately arises. If you see everything as separate from you, then it will manifest in that way in the Bardo.

Question: When you're very close to someone and they die and are going through the Bardo, are you in a way dragged through the Bardo with them?

Mark: Oh absolutely. They will see you anywhere from the third to the seventh day. After a while they will begin to lose track of you because the Bardo will become overwhelming. But if you were very close to them, like a husband or a wife to each other and you lived your life together, that relationship would of course be a strong element of what gets played out in the Bardo. People oftentimes report seeing loved ones when they move in the Bardo. In most cases they're seeing the thought-constructs of those people reflected in their own minds. All you ever see is what's in your own mind. If you want to see anything, look within yourself.

Question: Small children often have very bizarre internal fears. Images and things that are not being derived from what they've experienced since they've come into the world. Are those perhaps pieces of things that they've experienced in the Bardo and have carried in with them?

Mark: Yeah, that's my theory. In young people very fresh from the Bardo, the Bardo will immediately go subconscious and unconscious when they get born. They've just gone through this incredibly wild experience. Five days ago they were involved with the wrathful deities and then the last seven days they went through the womb gate and then the last nine months they were living inside the womb as they were gaining their body. It's an extremely stressful process and all of that goes unconscious as soon as the person hits the waking state. When you have a person who is very, very young and they're seeing supernatural beings, they're most likely seeing artifacts from the Bardo. The psychic element is wide open in almost all cases of children. It doesn't close down for some years so they naturally look directly in the hearts and minds of the humans around them. They don't have a template of judging it as good or bad, so they just accept it. In some cases a person will hang on to that through their life. In other cases the educational process and the system will slowly beat it out of them. With no spiritual training, no meditation and being told "It's just your imagination" and "Only believe what you see and hear", a person will just slowly shut those gates down and all of that stuff will become unconscious and subconscious data.

Question: I've heard a couple different versions of the Bodhisattva; I thought the promise was made by the individual who, in the moment of enlightenment, chooses to come back into this realm for the sake of everyone who is still here, and vows to keep coming back until everyone comes across. ("That's true," says Mark) In that case though, the person still has to fall back into the bottom of this realm and start from scratch forming their experience…

Mark: But there are different ways. Oftentimes if a person is advanced, they will go into a kind of holding – they've given the Bodhisattva vow, they've become Bodhisattvas, they've gained their own liberation but out of the nature of the Bodhisattva vow, even though they themselves are enlightened and liberated, they will return as a conscious action. In this case they will tend to go through a process of consciousness where they will enter the womb gate by sheer intent. A regular person is kind of driven into the womb gate, almost like an animal, just like being lashed by karmic cause and it is kind of a seeking of refuge from the tumult of the Bardo. A Bodhisattva will be much different. They will actually go through the consciousness transference into the universal state and then, out of the nature of the Bodhisattva vow, they will return with conscious intent and they will select the time and the place of their birth, they will select the womb, they will select the avenue of acting out of compassion, out of power, out of teaching, out of service. They will pick the perfect moment of birth to fulfill that karma. There's also a standard of progression levels between Bodhisattvas. Like the first time you come back as a Bodhisattva, it's like riding a horse. You can stay on the horse but it's ugly. Then as a person comes back many times they can make that move with incredible clarity, intensity and power. In other words, it's much smoother and less muss and fuss. Even the Bodhisattva return is subject to capabilities, conditions and connections.

Question: But nonetheless, they have to re-form their cognitive process all over again…

Mark: Yeah, they have to take on another body. What they'll tend to do is tag a body and stay out of the body until two minutes before the birth. A really advanced Bodhisattva will sit inside the mother's womb in meditation. If you did a sonogram on it, you would see the Bodhisattva sitting cross-legged. They are actually meditating and merged with the Great Light. The mother is basically in a state of bliss having wild dreams of advanced consciousness. In some cases when the newborn child emerges, it is painless for the mother and the newborn is completely enlightened, and will sometimes say hello. There are lots of different tales where advanced souls went through the rebirth process and produced very unusual moments at the moment of birth.

Question: Just like there will be individuals who at the age of three or four can sit down at the piano and immediately begin playing and obviously it's something they've brought with them but nonetheless their intellect and all their process of conceptualizing still has to be generated by what they can experience and access in their present life.

Mark: Yeah and what you're talking about is the Tulku system whereby if you're a Bodhisattva and you're moving up the ladder to being an advanced and powerful Bodhisattva, then you can perfectly choose the moment of your birth that will cause the greatest amount of effect on the avenue of dharma that you are selecting. Also if you are a Bodhisattva of some import, the enlightened sangha will manage the downloading of the new brain. They'll be right there. You hear of very dramatic examples like the Dalai Lama. Whenever he dies, he always writes a four-line poem that gives directions where to look for him in the next birth. He's already seen it before he's died – under a mountain of a certain shape, next to a tree, at a certain time – he'll call it the time of the snowbird or the snow leopard – he gives the exact time and place and then there's a team of guys who go and find him. As soon as they find him, instead of just letting him run around and be a regular kid, they snatch him and put him into a program to very effectively download all of the information of the new brain, leaving very little opportunity for mistake or leaving anything for random chance.

Even if you are a Bodhisattva of middling status, the enlightened sangha will look after you. They might not throw a net over you the first year of your life, but they'll look over you and guide your steps to your Guru. They'll cause events to occur so that your mind will be shaped in a certain way and you will meet your Guru and get Shaktipat at the soonest possible opportunity. It's relative to your importance – the time, the place, the connections and the conditions.

Question: And meanwhile each of us should be grateful for the fact that we can take you completely for granted, that when the moment comes and you're needed, you'll be there?

Mark: That's right. That's the contract. It's actually one of my highest levels of expertise. I'm good at it. It's not hard and that's one of the reasons we get together so often. What I need out of you, more than anything is for you to be calm. Don't panic. Relax and the best things will happen. If you start panicking, it's just like trying to save a drowning person. They won't calm down.

Question: The Bardo of Death and the Bardo of Life seem to be different in the speed of the way things happen.

Mark: The conditioning of the four envelopes of body, speech and mind – the physical, subtle physical, mental and supra causal envelopes produce an apparatus of apprehension that seems to separate cause and effect. Even though it seems to separate it, they still arise simultaneously. That's the Zen insight that the cause and the effect arise at the same time. As soon as you get used to that it gets easier and easier to spot it. You can see why a person is doing a thing because they're acting under the effect of a cause that is arising. The cause might be buried in their subconscious; the cause might even be buried in a previous incarnation but it's still the same moment. They can never be separated. Though when you take away the body, the body becomes the mandala. Take away the body and the mind and the death and after-death state – the power and drama of the death experience is that there is no separation between cause and effect. Everything happens simultaneously and instantaneously. That's why it's so overwhelming.

Question: Is there no consensus reality? Is this Bardo just like the Death Bardo in that it's all a construction of your thoughts? It's my single-person construction of thought not necessarily congruent or happening in anybody else's reality?

Mark: It's the perfect expression of the ocean of consciousness and the Creation. Here is the world, we see the world, we experience the firmness of the earth, the fluidity of water, the heat of fire – pervading it all is the scintillating ocean of consciousness. The physical activity in the world takes place in the envelope of activity, but to act in this world you have to have a body. If you don't have a body it doesn't affect the world in quite the same way. That's why Gurus bother to take bodies. But no, there is no suchness, there is no objectness to any of it; there is no thing, it's just consciousness.

It's an aggregate; it's an assembly of qualities. We've talked about imputed terms.

What's interesting about the human form is that it perfectly expresses the Bardo. It's a desirable form in that it expresses the Bardo with incredible intensity, both at its manifest level and its empty level and everything in between.

Question: The other thing you said was everything that comes to you is going to come to you. You can't stop it and you don't cause it.

Mark: You've already caused it. The arising of your life is a congruence of cause and effect. There's a part of you that is arising as cause and there's a part of you that is arising as effect at the same time. You're not all cause nor are you all effect. You are an aggregate of cause and effect so you are fulfilling the effect of previous cause generating new cause for future effect. They're all arising simultaneously. When you learn to stop the mind, the whole thing goes away. No cause, no effect and that's how you merge with the Great Light.

There's an implication of a wheel in cause and effect. Here's a cause "whoooosh", it must produce this effect which gives rise to a new cause, to effect, to cause, to effect, and thus you have the wheel of samsara. It has a kind of momentum and Creation is eternal, it never stops. At the same time the ocean of consciousness is present and void of nature, completely empty, beyond all qualities, without quality. Not even the quality of emptiness is present as a quality. It's possible to move your attention into that spectrum and everything becomes empty. If there were objectness to the world, if it had its own truth, it would never end.

Question: So as long as you don't get attached to the fruit of your action, whatever is going to come to you is going to come to you anyway, so it's not really relevant what you do or don't do.

Mark: That's true. The effect of placing one's attention into the void nature of emptiness gives rise to the contact with emptiness and the transference of consciousness to the Great Light occurs. Whatever you place your attention on is what happens. If you place your attention on the Great Light, it is the Great Light that manifests. You've already set X amount of cause in motion. You could decide to produce no more cause. "I'm just going to live out the effects. I'm going to place all my new cause in the Great Light." That means that the effect is on a finite cycle. It's only going to go around so many times and then you're going to run out of causes. What's going to happen? You'll just disappear.

You'll merge into the Great Light.

In a way that's what we're doing. We are beginning to act in such a way that we produce no cause. Now all our present and future cause terminates in the Great Light. We place no cause that will terminate in the world, thus the effects that are playing out now are of a finite number and as that all unravels under the pressure of shaktipat, there's a point where there's no more cause and your consciousness will transfer to the Great Light. And then your body and your mind will be an effect of the Great Light. That's what it's like when you're around a Nityananda. You can see his body, but he has no cause of any human nature. His only cause is of the Great Light itself.

Question: So let's say one day I take everything too seriously, get angry and then later understand why I got angry and work through that. Would I still need to work through that initial anger even though I saw it and got understanding about it?

Mark: It'll produce an artifact, a karmic seed. The next thing you want to do is produce an artifact of its opposite. If you produce anger then you'll want to produce the opposite of anger, which is love and patience. So you produce two countervailing causes that offset each other. You're attached to none of them and offer all three of the seeds to God and the Guru and they will be absorbed. They won't settle in your system. Produce the expiation – as you said, seeing that you made a mistake – produce remorse for having made that mistake, causing harm to yourself and another, resolve not to do it again, and you've produced a condition where the cause will be neutralized.

Question: Is there a time component between that? Let's say that I get angry and six hours, six months, two years later I'm able to process that and then develop the loving feeling…

Mark: The faster the better. If you can do it in six hours, that's best. If you allow it to settle into the system it will subtly, subconsciously exert a conditional pressure on you because it will exist as a karmic seed. Because it's there it will subtly exert its effect. It's very interesting, when you look at a person and you apprehend all of the qualities of their body, how their body looks, how their face looks, you feel the quality of their mind – you can feel what they've thought about. If they're an angry person, that anger has actually shaped the lines of their face, shaped the quality of their body. You can see the anger in the tissues and the existence of anger produces a momentum that will generate the likelihood of more anger. That's why you want to produce a neutrality. If you find yourself getting angry you want to recognize it and neutralize it as fast as possible so it doesn't produce a karmic seed in your continuum because it has a weight. It will weigh you down. Those seeds that you generated before shaktipat will have been in there and some of them you will have worked out. Such as you're going along and you have a run of bad luck. You get sick and maybe somebody breaks into your car. What that's about is the playing out of maybe the fifty times you got angry and produced a weight that produced a negative activity. It's in your mind stream and it manifests karma as something of the feeling tone of that anger.

Question: You had said that generally speaking about 49 days after death, that one is reincarnated, re-embodied? ("Yes, generally speaking", says Mark) How does that work then if I'm with somebody and their cousin walks by who died two years ago? How do we see the ghosts and things like that if they've already reincarnated?

Mark: Because we share the same blood with our family, consciousness infuses into the blood and it's very possible to see people in the afterlife. In some cases due to karmic conditions where they will be in a suspended Bardo for a period of time before their reincarnation, it can be a few years in some cases.

Also maybe they have reincarnated and they're thinking of you on a subconscious level and you will see them in their old mind form.

I've seen lots of people that I've known die and I've felt them go through the Bardo, I've felt them either reincarnate or go into paradisiacal states. If they were advanced people they would go into the upper paradisiacal states for a period of time and then they would normally reincarnate and I would feel them and now I feel them in the world and see them in my mind's eye as young children being reborn.

One of the Bardo realms is to become a ghost. If people disincarnate negatively, misunderstand the process of disincarnation, death and reincarnation, exit the gate of the hungry ghosts, they'll exit out the gate of the mouth and enter into the world of the pretas and move around the world in the form of a ghost. It happens especially if the person died around negative conditions of intense emotional confusion and affliction. So it can be any of those conditions.

Question: Sometimes when a woman is pregnant and a higher Guru or someone else goes into the womb (as a rebirth) and meditates and the mother feels the advanced consciousness, does she herself reach higher levels as well?

Mark: Oh absolutely. She'll experience it like a darshan, being in the presence of an enlightened person. Because the being would be physically inside the parameters of her body, she would experience states of bliss and have dreams of the highest states because she would be offering her body as a gateway to an advanced soul. The advanced soul would take complete care of her and probably guarantee her enlightenment as she lived out her karma as the mother. Oftentimes the agreements between advanced souls and those souls that serve as mother and father are arrangements of long standing. You'll oftentimes see around powerful teachers, beings seeking the darshan of the teachers through the womb gates of the female members of the sangha. Sometimes you'll see the same soul go through the same womb several times, working out the relationship with the mother and the higher soul, working out karma. The equation of karma, conditions and connections is very complex. You just see everything. People get themselves in all kinds of situations.

Question: You've mentioned a million times since I've been studying with you that this world is the Bardo of Death and how you handle this place is how you handle the Bardo and the idea thinking that you can create different constructs there than you have here is pretty bizarre.

Mark: Exactly so, exactly so. As you live, so will you die. This Bardo of Life and the Bardo of Death are the same. It just unfolds. If you understand that, then you will act accordingly. If you take the Bardo of Life and operate in the echelons of dharma and higher dharma and highest dharma, then your death will be an expression of the highest dharma. If you take your life and you go down this road and that road and you indulge in every reckless feeling and sensation and indulge in the poisons whenever you feel like it, that also will be reflected at the moment of truth, which is the moment of death. They are not different. It's an idea that is difficult for Westerners to grasp because our minds tend to be linear. We tend to think that we start here and go down a line and we end here. The end and the beginning are the same.

Question: What's so clear from your explanation is that physiologically it's identical. In essence our life is a composition of our karmas playing out and we're forced to deal with them and then you die and the karmas that have accrued through that life are then played out. Then in the Bardo you're forced to deal with them again. It's basically the same exact thing only there's the acceleration. Is that really it?

Mark: Acceleration of terms. Again, it's imputed terms and at any moment if you realize the truth in the living Bardo, you merge with the Great Light. If you wait until the moment of death and realize the truth in the Bardo after death, you merge with the Great Light. If you refuse to recognize the Great Light in the Bardo after death, what do you do? You go into the cycle of rebirth. The karma that you have been so attached to, that you have refused to let go of, the countless opportunities through the entire 49-day Bardo, become the terms of your new birth. Likewise, if you realized the Great Light and you are a great soul in the form of a Bodhisattva and have promised to be reborn even though you yourself have achieved your own liberation, your own enlightenment, then you can be reborn on those terms as well. So anything is possible.

Question: What's the story with actors and even writers, people who are out there going on stage and going through all these horrible emotions and murdering people and going through anger and hatred?

Mark: The brain does not recognize the difference between acting and doing it for real. As far as the brain is concerned, it's happening.

Question: So those actors are screwed when they go through the Bardo?

Mark: It's a wild art form. And yes, they should think twice.

Question: What about writers, when you're just intellectually…

Mark: They're even worse. (Laughter) No, it's interesting because writers are imagining and producing a schematic for other people. When we watch a play or a movie, we see people play out. When we read, we take our own experience and we produce a schematic that reflects that story. All of art is an opportunity, a laboratory, to express truths. You produce a scenario wherein truth can be found in its highest form.

Question: Are the karmas different then between imagining something and actually trying to experience it?

Mark: It would be what the intent is.

Question: Their intent was to help other people experience different things. Is that the out then for actors, what their intent was?

Mark: If their intent is that, that will be the karmic effect. They will have the karmic seeds. The best actors use what they call method acting, where they produce the frequency within themselves. Their bodies are their instruments; their minds are their instruments and when you see great actors, they're not just making their face into a certain shape or moving their body, they're producing the frequencies and you have that experience. It's incredibly powerful. They're not very many people who can actually do it.

Question: So it's only the Oscar winners who are going to Hell?

Mark: Exactly. (Laughter)

Question: When you become a character as you're acting and you're done with your performance and you ground yourself out, then you don't take that character into your life after the performance. You leave that character behind and it should be fine. Right?

Mark: It leaves an impression inside your system. It's like going through an experience. Like last week you got into a fender bender and you got into an intense argument and you felt really strange all day after the argument and you even feel weird the next day and then the day after that it kind of gets better and by the third or fourth day, you've forgotten about it. But the fact that you got into the argument and the guy yelled at you and you yelled at him and he threatened you and you threatened him back, you've produced karma. There was a chemical reaction in the brain that produced a karmic artifact that will play out in the Bardo.

Did you ever see the movie "What the Bleep Do We Know?" One of the points that was so interesting in that movie was that the brain does not recognize the difference between acting something out and having it happen for real. The brain chemistry just builds it and experiences it and that produces the karmic detritus, the karmic artifact. You'll oftentimes see artists, especially actors, kind of become unglued in their lives because they pretend so many things that their system in the end can't balance, their system becomes overwhelmed and they just kind of come unglued over a period of time. Sometimes you'll see men hang in longer because their nervous systems are a little more rugged. You watch female actors and if you see them do a series of really intense roles, then you see them four years later, they look like they've aged fifteen years because they've done this to themselves, and their systems are so open and subject to that effect. It's very open; it's very direct.

Question: But when you ground yourself out after your performances, you don't have that effect on your body. Is that right?

Mark: That's very important. Some people have that skill to some degree and some people have it to a lesser degree. I watch a lot of movies and I watch actors very intensely for this very reason. I find it very interesting. I see the people who are good at cycling it – they do better, last longer and hold on to their health. The ones that have a shaky underlying psychology, their lives become confused. They tend to lose their moral center and oscillate over into a very wild way of life that is destructive in many ways. I think one of the reasons why you see actors constantly marrying and remarrying is a desperate attempt to try to produce some kind of grounding experience in their lives. It's a search for truth and thus it has a price.

Those of you who are actors, actresses, writers, artists of any kind – the resolution remains the same. Recognize the void nature of appearance, see the underlying emptiness and recognize the Great Light present in the Creation. My experience in art is: that is the attempt, and whatever form it takes to bring about an expression that reveals a truth that is beyond condition and can be recognized by anyone at any time, it's hard to do.

Question: When we sit with you and go through these events and you're clearing karma from the 100 fibers that move between the base of the spine and the crown of the head, as those get more and more empty, when the death process happens and you start going through a series of events, can you recognize what is happening and choose to move through the Bardo consciously knowing that it's empty? ("Absolutely", says Mark) Almost as an act of will to just intentionally go through every step?

Mark: You can travel the Bardo inside the body. You don't have to wait until death.

Question: Oh great, it's almost like the map is within us even when we have the body so that we don't necessarily have to wait until we don't have a body?

Mark: Advanced meditation is just that. Realizing the map. For the advanced soul, by the time they come to the moment of death, they would have completely realized the map of the Bardo so their Bardo event would be an act of enlightenment.

Question: Do you have to consciously be aware that you are actually transversing the Bardo in order to be doing it?

Mark: Absolutely not. You're transversing the Bardo, period. That's what's happening at all times. We did it Saturday and that was an awakened act. We traveled the entire Bardo in the course of six or seven hours.

Question: I find it very fascinating that because this is all wired into us, it's like you are actually becoming more yourself, your higher Self. So you don't really have to be doing anything other than being yourself.

Mark: It manifests at the physical, subtle physical, causal and supra causal levels. You're awakening to your true nature, your true Self. You are your true Self, but part of it is conscious and part of it is unconscious. The awakening factor is in how that aspect of Self that you are unconscious to becomes conscious. That's the fruit of the spiritual practices involving the plunge of meditation and learning to see into the unseen. That's what they call the holy dharma.

Question: It seems cool because you're basically transmitting this map constantly everywhere you go, everything you do, you're just broadcasting, "This is the way."

Mark: That's what a teacher does, teaching you the map, showing you the way. And there is a way.
Question: And the way can incorporate any degree of wildness or any given set of situations or like you said, people's lives are the aggregate. Right?

Mark: In the end it's an assembly of qualities of an individual. There will be arcs of extremes in all directions and then there is the dynamic of the whole at the center. Like the Buddhist said, the middle path, which tends to fall away from the extremes and generate strength at the center, produces the illumination that overwhelms and overrides all conditions.

Question: And it's cool because the frequency of emptiness can immediately dissolve all of those attractions or all of those things that are binding.

Mark: Absolutely. And that's the feature of recognition. If you recognize it as empty and see it as empty, which is a subtle action, then it is apprehended as such.

Question: So no matter how crazy or seemingly impossible a situation is…

Mark: That's the thesis of the wrathful deities because you're dealing with something very extreme and the tendency in that situation is to believe it to be real because of its force, but if you recognize its emptiness, it becomes empty.

Question: Are there beings that put themselves intentionally into the most extreme situations imaginable?

Mark: Certainly. As you awaken you go through

phases of high adventure and in any given life you'll have enough steam in you to go through some very intense adventures – go into dangerous places where darkness is very rampant or places where power is at an extreme level. There are different levels of power, different conditions. That's part of the fun side of the Bardo as you awaken to it. You can go quite literally to different universes. Live out multiple lives in those places. You don't have to just stay here on one planet with one set of conditions.

Question: You've said before that the Guru often appears in really dire situations like wars and strife…

Mark: Yes, absolutely. The enlightened sangha deals like a contract with people and people get themselves in all kind of conditions and those conditions unfold and you go where the conditions arise.

Question: Would you like to share with us your future plans?

Mark: Well, there's a time and place for everything.

EXCERPTS FROM THE Q & A SATSANG ~ OCTOBER 30, 2001

Question: You said that all living beings tremble before death. You go into Nirvikalpa Samadhi so you're not really in the same class of living beings as humans. What happens with you?

Mark: I've actually gone through the death process a number of times. Advanced meditation is death, and as you go back and forth along that track you iron out the neurotic fear of the event. That doesn't mean it's not a tricky moment, but you're not afraid. Also, it doesn't mean that you're not going to regret being parted from the beautiful things that happened to you in a given life. Life is sweet indeed.

Question: So it's still tricky for the Dalai Lama or the guy that's done it a dozen times?

Mark: Well, you want a specific result, and that

requires precise action.

Question: When you die, is it like when you faint? Is it that same kind of feeling?

Mark: No. It's different. One of the things about it is you are completely self-possessed at the moment of death. It's not like you're slipping away; you're becoming yourself.

Question: So if you know you are about to die, if you call the Guru in this world, the Guru comes?

Mark: Yeah, and the Guru will help you as much as you can be helped. It is an extremely personal event and it's important that you experience everything. There's nothing to be afraid of. I want to get away from the whole fear model. It's really high adventure and it's really intense but it's nothing to be afraid of.

Question: Mark, have you picked out where you're going next?

Mark: Yeah.

Question: Is there any chance of your letting us know where that area is or teaching us a way to get there?

Mark: Yeah, there is a chance. As soon as you are able to learn it, I will teach you. There are times where, in advanced speech, I've shown all of you maps. It will be information you will be able to access when you're ready to access it.

Question: How does a relationship with a Guru interact with your death?

Mark: If you call on the Guru at the moment of death, the Guru will show up. If you're confused, he'll inform you that you've died. He'll produce an illusion where you are transported into a condition of liberation and delivered from the wheel of samsara. Through the power of the grace of the Guru and the grace of the lineage, your consciousness principle will be wrapped up and delivered from the power of the wheel. It's just like Virgil guiding Danté through the Netherworld, but it's very fast. As a rule, because death is recognized as a tricky moment, the Guru will go for the best path, as fast as possible, without taking any chances.

The point of a lifetime relationship with a Guru is to learn to trust him. Then when you're at the moment of death and the Guru starts doing things, you are relaxed. You trust what's going to happen; you accept it as the Guru's grace. You go along with it rather than resist to the last second. That's a conversation that takes place between the Guru and the disciple.

Question: You've said that entering the death Bardo is just like being here in this room. What does that mean?

Mark: The mind keeps assembling appearances, which is another reason they say you die as you live. The dream that you had with you in life is the dream you take with you in death.

Question: Wouldn't you look at your own body and think, "Oh, I must be dead because I am seeing my body lying there"?

Mark: It will flicker by your mind, but then your mind will produce a dream. Your dead body will make sense in the dream. Maybe in the Bardo after you die, you'll go to sleep, and you'll dream you saw your body. You'll think, "Oh, that's kind of strange." You'll feel odd, but then the next thing will happen and you'll go on just like you do in life now. For example, what do you do when you get up in the morning? You think, "Oh, I'm going to have my tea." You have your tea and ask, "What do I have to do today?" You're off on your errands. Then it's lunch and then you'll just come up with the next thing after lunch. Even after death, in the

Bardo you're doing the exact same thing. But it happens faster and faster. Just when your mind is about to stop, what do you do? You come up with something to do.

Question: But gradually those things stop working?

Mark: That's what occurs.

Question: What happens if you miss your shot at entering into the infinite ocean of light and becoming liberated?

Mark: The fabric of all your karma of this life and past lives becomes the content of the movie you then start spinning. The first three days of the Bardo are like a vacation, and again, it varies with each person. This period is basically just like life in a way; you dream the dreams of being alive. It's one of the jokes on human nature that most people don't know they've died for two or three days. But right away the truth is being revealed. You'll see loved ones, first in ideal settings and then mourning your loss. Then you'll start to see their mental projections as well as your own mental projections. The clues start pouring in. You notice that the edge of your reality is decaying and then realize, "Oh... I died." After that the winds of the Bardo begin to blow and start to drive the soul.

It's like the movie *Jacob's Ladder*; the main character starts receiving hints from both benign and demonic beings. It took him the whole movie to finally figure out he was dead and only needed to let go. The whole process took place over the course of a week in a seeming life but it was all a Bardo dream.

If a person has a very strong desire that went unfulfilled in life, they may have enough power to resist the winds of the Bardo. They refuse to enter the Bardo and become a hungry ghost instead. They have enough power to stay in the world and walk around. They can see the objects of their desire but they can't fulfill them because they don't have a body. They'll haunt an area or follow people around, feeding on other people's energy. They try to use this mental energy to reproduce a reality but it never works. They feel excessively embittered and that's why they don't just stay ghosts. They're called 'hungry ghosts' because they possess a wild, hysterical bitterness since they haven't been able to fulfill a single desire for a long period of time. You don't want that to happen to you.

Question: What if I were to miss the moment of liberation and wind up in the three days. Then beings show up for the final call with the winds blowing and I'm saying, "Oh no, I'm not going." What happens if I end up missing the last bus off Devil's Island?

Mark: There are a series of five lights that are the elemental basis and they're the wrong doorways. They lead to rebirth. There's one light that leads to liberation. The light of the Self appears as the light of ten billion suns. It leads to liberation and happens instantaneously. Anyone can access it but almost everybody misses it. It's so bright and fast that people tend to shy away from it, sensing it as a form of obstruction. The multiple lights come after the light of liberation. These are the basic lights of the elements and the senses and are all leading to rebirth. But then there's a moment at the end of that sequence where the light of the Self appears again.

The best thing in approaching death is to have meditated enough so that you've heard the footsteps of death coming. When death strikes, you will know what it is. Even as you're dying, you'll know you're dying, and you'll sit up and go into the best meditation you can. You'll start noticing that it's very easy to draw all of your consciousness into the sushumna because that's where it wants to go. So instead of becoming frightened, you'll say, "Oh, I'm just meditating and I've done this a thousand times in a thousand meditations. I'm just going along with it."

As death happens, a powerful drama takes place. You feel a subtle regret because you know that everything is happening for the last time. You're not going to be allowed to come back to this house ever again. You're not going to see your loved ones ever again, at least not in this form or this setting. Get used to the idea of transience so you don't linger over that last regret too long. Death is a very tricky moment and you need the best attention you can muster.

Question: It's kind of like a reverse dark night of the soul?

Mark: Yes, it is. When death happens, it clicks along really fast. Now, if you are aware, what seems like winds to other people won't to you. It's just like a doorway. You just walk up to it and you say, "Ah, no, I don't want to step through that doorway." You go up to another one and go, "Ah, no I don't want to step through that one." At the same time you should think, "You know, I'm dying. OK – I should call my Guru." You call on the Guru internally, and he'll show up.

CHAPTER 10

Weekly Meeting
~ Meditation on the Bardo and Bodhicitta ~
March 13, 2007

The term Bardo Thodol means the interval that enlightens upon contact. The Bardo Thodol is said to be a space between life and death, oftentimes referred to as the intermediate state. The startling idea that this extends to is that life and death are the same – that it is the movement of consciousness through the architecture of the human form in life and that there is a moment in life where the mind is separated from the body. This is the moment we call death. But there is a dramatic event that takes place between life and death that is an interval where the consciousness is in transformation.

In life consciousness is sheathed inside the body. The interval of the Bardo Thodol is the sheering away of the physical body leaving the pure consciousness completely revealed and liberated. The body falls away and only the consciousness is present and the process that we call death is this separation. The movement of consciousness through the architecture of the human form takes place in such a way that the consciousness surges forward with incredible force. But what is present inside this architecture is stored in all of the qualities of life. We've all heard that at the moment of death our life plays out and we see every single moment of our life. And that is essentially all of the stored memory of this incarnation basically dumping into the consciousness.

We come to understand that most important in this is the central nerve, the sushumna, which is a nerve that conducts the entire essence of the aggregate of experience from the physical body, to the memory, to the senses, to the mind, to the soul. We're speaking in terms of the metaphysics of the human form. The soul is understood to be the aggregate of the four bodies. The central nerve flows from the crown of the head to the base of the spine. The left and right are the female and male energies. On the right are the male energies called pingala. They're white in nature. On the left are the feminine energies called ida. They're red in color. Suspended along these three rivers or streams of consciousness are six wheels called chakras and they are placed at the base of the spine, the loins, the navel, the heart, the throat and the forehead. There's also a chakra at the crown of the head that has 1000 petals. The chakra at the base of the spine has four streams; at the genital region, six; at the navel, ten; at the heart, twelve; at the throat, sixteen; at the forehead, two; and again, at the crown of the head, 1000.

These six chakras and their subtle nadis add up to 50 and they're said to be 50 yang energies, or male energies, which flow in the right side in the white channel and 50 feminine energies that flow in the left side, in the red channel. This adds up to 100. In the spiritual understanding of the human architecture, these 100 fibers contain the totality of being. They run the senses, memory and mind. They are relative to the physical spine and in the subtle physical body they are in the energy field. They are like a subtle physical ganglion. All of these fibers terminate in the brain. They break out into 42 peaceful deities or fibers that conduct energy that emanates from the heart center and 58 wrathful energies that originate in the brain. In the death process all of the layers of consciousness dissolve one into another until they get down into the central nerve and express themselves in each of these six chakras and fire along these 50 and 50 fibers, reducing themselves to the essence of the essence of the essence of your consciousness. In other words, every single thought-construct that you've had, either consciously, subconsciously or unconsciously, is stored in the ganglion of the brain, spinal cord and nervous system in this subtle physical system called the 100 fibers.

In the Bardo Thodol they are called the 100 Deities of the Interval Between Life and Death. These 100 deities again are divided between the yang and yin energies. The red energies are stored in the navel region. The white energies are stored in the upper brain. The moment of truth when the body dies takes place at the instant the breath stops. When this process of the separation of consciousness of mind and body known as death occurs, in that moment the Great Light of the ocean of consciousness appears. This light has been pervading our consciousness, our mind, our body, our heart and our entire being, for the totality of our life; however, the drama of our existence has acted like the projection of a movie across the screen of our lives. All our feelings, all our thoughts and all of our actions are projected across this screen, and it is the force of our life with this light that produces the feeling of being alive. At the moment of death, that apparition is stripped away and only the underlying consciousness remains.

The quality of this light is the nature of enlightenment, it is the nature of pure consciousness, it is the infinite light, it is the ocean of consciousness, it is God, regardless of our concept of God that has emerged in any given life, as the fruit of the time and the space and the culture through which we lived. And whatever that concept is, it is the connection to your life. At the moment of death this Great Light emerges with great force.

Everytime when we meet we always open with a meditation called 'Raising Bodhicitta'. I want to connect our meditation tonight with the true underlying meaning of the Bodhicitta and tie it into the discussion we've been having the past weeks on the profound subject of the Bardo. At the beginning of the meditation I ask everyone to raise Bodhicitta. The word Bodhicitta means enlightened mind. As an act of will, an act of love, we raise the attention, the enlightened aspect of our own consciousness, of our own being. We set aside the thoughts and involvement with the external world and we go into the essence of ourselves and we touch that light which is present. This is the core of spiritual training, the core of meditation. It is the ability – as an act of attention – to separate our attention from the external expression of the entanglement of our senses, which are a subtle expression of our mind, our desires and our conditioning, and touch the Great Light. We raise the Bodhicitta, the enlightened mind.

We've also discussed that the enlightened mind, the Bodhicitta, assembles with great force at the crown of the head. At the crown of the head it turns into the White Bodhicitta. This is the place where the atmosphere of the enlightened mind and the individual mind form what is spoken of as a drop of pure consciousness. It is where the ocean of consciousness churns and becomes the individual person. In the human being, life infuses into the body at the crown of the head. It is also the doorway of the exit of life out of the body. It's very important to understand that, as it is the most auspicious gate of exit.

The red energies are stored in the lower spine in the region of the navel, the seat of the fire element, the force of the Creation. One of the aspects of the meditation called Raising Bodhicitta is the arousal of the Bodhicitta at the crown of the head – the White Bodhicitta at the crown of the head and the Red Bodhicitta at the navel and causing the White Bodhicitta to drop down to the crown of the head, down through the center of the brain, along the track of the sushumna and into the heart where it is held. At the same time arouse the energy of the MahaKundalini, which exists in the form of the coiled serpent in the position at the base of the spine beneath the root chakra. The birth of the Kundalini gives the presence of what is called the *tigle*, the fire of life, the fire of the Creation that is stored at the navel.

One of the most mystical aspects of the Bodhicitta is the ability to isolate with one's attention the White Bodhicitta and cause it to move from its seat at the crown of the head down into the seat of the heart. At the same time giving rise to the Red Bodhicitta, raising it up, causing it to join at the heart region. This can be done while still in the body, while still in the living reflex of the Bardo Thodol.

We understand that the heart region is said to be the seat of the Bodhicitta. It is the one point inside the structure of the human form where all four bodies intersect at the base of the breast bone– physical, subtle physical, causal and supra causal. If you feel the base of your breastbone and go down about the width of one finger and back towards the center of the body, there's a subtle space there. This is the seat of the Bodhicitta.

One of the most powerful meditations of enlightenment is the bringing of the drop of the White Bodhicitta and the drop of the Red Bodhicitta to the seat of the Bodhicitta at the region of the heart. The energy of the enlightened white and red energies will pervade the four bodies and produce a direct connection with the Great Light, the ocean of consciousness, while in the body. At the moment of truth when the mind and the body are separated, if you have raised Bodhicitta everyday in your life, in the drama, confusion, fear and emotion of the last moment of life, you will be able to raise Bodhicitta in exactly the same way and gain complete liberation, gain complete enlightenment.

The understanding of the Bardo Thodol is in the

translation of the words 'Bardo Thodol' – the intermediate state that enlightens upon contact, if understood, if realized.

There's a lot of intense theory and very intense metaphysics in the discussion of the Bardo Thodol, but tonight what I wanted to do is bring into focus this meditation of arousing Bodhicitta that we open every session of meditation. What's the first thing we do? We raise Bodhicitta. I want to make the point of the connection of this sadhana, raising Bodhicitta, and align it with the true meaning of life and death and the interval of the intermediate state.

As we begin meditating we begin the cycling of the deep bellows breathing. This is the deep breathing that is controlled by the solar plexus. The expansion of the solar plexus draws the breath in; the compression of the solar plexus pushes the breath out. Listen to the sound of the breath – it carries the vibration of the SoHam. Pay attention to the space between the breaths.

Now in life when we breathe in we expect to breathe out. In life when we breathe out we expect to breathe in. What is it that I always say? Focus your meditation on the space between the breaths because now you have the luxury to expect to breathe out when you breathe in. I'm telling you now, there will come a moment…you will breathe in but you will not breathe out or you will breathe out but you will not breathe in. It is the interval between the two breaths out of which the Bardo Thodol will emerge. Press your attention in the space between the breaths. Listen to the sound. Now everyone please give rise to the Bodhicitta. We will begin…

CHAPTER 11

Excerpts from Questions and Answers
Joshua Tree Summer Retreat
June 22, 2008

Question: When you die and you no longer have a physical body, are you dealing with the exact same subtle architecture of the human form as you've described it to us, the sushumna, the chakras, etc? So you just keep working with all that stuff or does something shift when you die?

Mark: It shifts, but it depends. If the person is an advanced yogi, they go into Samadhi. They can enter the condition of death, sheer the body off, and enter into the awakened condition with pretty much the totality of the relative body, the mental body, and the universal body. That is why beings like Muktananda and Bhagawan

Nityananda – as an act of freedom – can remain in existence throughout eternity and not merge. You maintain all of the fluidity of the body of light which is infinitely variable and can produce from a thousand to ten thousand different incarnations simultaneously. When that kind of incarnation is operating at full bore it can actually manifest and operate ten thousand physical bodies throughout a world system, or multiple world systems, going through the entire Bardo of life and death, the interval between life and death. It's actually just an interval. The space between embodiment and disembodiment is just a space. Life and death are exactly the same thing with an interval between them. And the conditions of the envelope shift.

The body falls away. That's its karma. It is usually a karmic condition that strikes the body either through an affliction of calamity, disease or decay, and then the life force will recede into increasingly subtle systems. It will go through the elemental systems. All the chakras are based on elemental centers of assembly, of cohesion. Those produce the array of lights that we hear about in the Bardo. They're the various gates. And also "The Great Light of the Billion Suns" appears, which actually enters from the crown of the head. All of the magnetic lights are organized to the various holes of the body. The advice is to ignore all of the lights and merge with the great light.

As you go through that process that system is kind of torn apart through the bardo process. First you go through the specific deities which is where one relives one's life and feels the exact weight and balance of every action. This takes place in the first six days.

On the seventh day comes the judgment. The judgment is, "Do you believe in the body? Do you think you were the Self, or did you really think you were a separate identity?" If you say, "I am a separate identity and I am seeking refuge" – which is the wrong thing to say – then the second stage of the Bardo comes. This is called "The Wrathful Deities", and the wrathful deities come in and they rip you apart. They rip apart the assembly of dearly held life force and the structure of the subtle body, and you are reduced to mind. That's not so bad except that if the mind is disorganized you don't have any filters. Right now your mind is filtered by the movement of the physical body, and the movement of the subtle physical body and all of the elemental bases. So you don't really notice that every thought arises instantaneously and every thought bears fruit instantaneously. It seems like there's a distance. You have the thought and then there's the illusion of time and then the fruit bears out. That's because you're in the envelope of the physical creation. But as you are extracted from the envelope of physical creation, you come to understand that the mind and the experience of the thought of the mind are exactly the same thing.

Now if you are an organized mind you will shun the darker and afflictive thoughts and give rise to a powerful organization of mind, and again seek the connection to the great light. But if you are a disorganized mind, you will experience the characterization of the wrathful deities as a time of terror because the mind is seeking refuge, and throwing out every desire of refuge one after another. It's just one trap after another because the mind produces the entire refuge and then you fall into their tap and then they come in and they rip that apart and you're frustrated again and you're driven further down, and driven further down. Every time that happens you're more disorganized, and more terrified. That lasts approximately fourteen to twenty days.

After the end of the nineteenth day the third phase of experience begins, which is just pure terror and desolation. You seek any refuge. And this is the beginning of the process of the rebirth and seeking a womb-gate. And so you go through that process and you begin to see all of your future mothers and fathers. A very complex algorithm takes place based on who and what you are, your karmic connection, and what you want, what you were and what you will be. And you're drawn through a womb-gate, and there you hatch and re-enter the world.

Question: When you don't have a body do you breathe?

Mark: There is a mental image just like in the movie "The Matrix" that survives to some extent, but as the mind becomes more disorganized under the constant attack of the wrathful deities that image changes, and changes, and changes, and changes to the point where you wouldn't recognize yourself because your mind is in a completely desperate state.

Question: So there is not a sense of something like infinite ocean flowing in and out like a universal prana that permeates your existence?

Mark: If you have practiced the SoHam mantra every day of your life for the last thirty years, you will be organized enough to produce the SoHam in the Bardo. That alone will produce deliverance. You will merge with the great light. The mantra will draw the great light. It will draw the Guru. The thrall of the Bardo will be shattered. The Guru will basically give you that ten seconds that you need to pull yourself together and he'll just draw you through and out. There is a whole sequence of operations based on how much sadhanna you've done, the connection to the Guru. It's very direct, very personal.

Question: Is there an unbroken sense of "I am" through that whole process?

Mark: Well let me put it another way – the reason you meditate every day of your life is so at the moment of your death you'll be able to concentrate and arise as an Enlightened being. If you become super organized you can do it even in this body. This is where that relationship with your spiritual training comes in. Having done it in this body, you've learned to organize yourself for precisely that moment. It's a tricky moment because if you come all apart, you become unglued, and you're gonna make a mess for yourself.

Question: Can you play with desire in this life time with the idea that you know at that final moment you can say "done, ready to go." Or is that kind of a dangerous game?

Mark: It's a dangerous game because it's fire. Desire is fire, and playing with fire is always dangerous. The formula of spiritual life is always very simple. Simplify the life, withdraw as much as possible – if not totally – from desire. Seek enlightenment. You're trying to strip down the impressions that you are generating because at the moment of death everything surges in. You're acting one way on the outside and you've got all these secret desires on the inside. The secret desires are not going to be secret at the moment of death. They will have their play. And so the idea of the spiritual training in life is facing the condition with very clear eyes. That's what is implicit in spiritual training. Usually you see it in people that have gone through enough incarnations that they have begun to spot the pattern. And they are interested in an alternative.

Question: Most people don't have the opportunity to control their death process so does it matter if it's accidental death, degenerative decay or intentional death?

Mark: Yes it matters. Sudden accidental death is much more difficult because it's better to be able to prepare. Again I say, it's a very tricky moment and even though you've trained your whole life you have to hold the line and not lose your equilibrium when the Vajra army comes for you. And there are a lot of reasons to be upset and to be frightened. When the Great Light appears, it feels like a sun exploding in front of you. If you think it's a nuclear bomb that's going to destroy you, you will turn and run into the Bardo. So you have to remind yourself to embrace that light when it comes. Know it's coming. Know that light is God. Know that light is the Guru.

How death comes is the exact karmic equilibrium of life. When people are driving down the road and they think they're going to work and instead they die in a car accident or a plane wreck or any kind of thing like that where you have very little time to organize yourself – you're plunged into the Bardo; it's violent. You're dealing with the drama of a very violent death and the confusion of the impressions of the death process and the onslaught of the drama can blend themselves and produce an unstable entry into the Bardo. Interestingly enough, in situations of war, you don't expect to live and so when death comes, it's very sudden, but you knew that your chances of living through the situation were not that high. It's a matter of light and some people go through an entire war without getting so much as a scratch. Some people get killed the first couple of weeks they're there. In all levels of those kind of situations, there's a little bit of expectation there.

One of the things about meditation is that you make a friend of the life force. Death doesn't come from out of the sky. Your death is with you every day of your life. Life and death are two sides of the same coin. And if you get very still and look inside yourself, you'll see death there waiting. You can see where it's already present. It often takes on the form of a kind of frozen not-life and everybody that has gone through the aging process to any degree is familiar with that presence. You just feel a part of the life force that is not available to you. It's been taken away from you. As you age, things get taken away from you and that's death talking to you right there. And if you listen closely there's likely a little warning that death is coming. Even if it's just a moment, that's all you need.

The best thing to do when you know you're dying is to sit upright. If your spine is horizontal on the ground, the gravity of the Earth will confuse the passage of the life force through the nerves. The idea of vertical is important. The movement from life into death is the withdrawal of life from the outer extremities coiled into the center. You feel the life force kind of roll up from the feet, up like a tube of toothpaste and enter into the sushumna, ida, pingala, outer nadis and the six gates. Once you get into the sushumna, you just want to fly straight up and out of the crown of your head like a bird through a skylight – as swift as possible, like an arrow. And you'll meet the great light and it will be gone. The great Yogis will always hear it coming and they will immediately just organize themselves and withdraw everything into the sushumna and will merge into Samadhi. They leave one step ahead of death. It's kind of like getting to the front of a mob and looking like you're leading a parade. It's going to happen anyway so you deal with it in a positive way.

Being alone is best. Often times people die surrounded by loved ones and family. It's better to be alone. Your concentration is better but it depends on how you are. Maybe for you it's easier if you are surrounded by all the signs of life, but what it will tend to do is be a distracting moment and you really need all your concentration. It's also important that nobody touch you while you go through the death process because the death process is extremely magnetic and if you're at the exact moment of making subtle and powerful moves within and you're touched externally, the energy goes "zzzzzzz" out to the touch and your attention will be divided in some way. So it's best to just find a moment off by yourself and take care of what you have to take care of. Pick your moment if possible.

Question: I had two friends recently who were ill who chose to self-exit, and I found it very disturbing at first, and yet I understand that they were trying to control their death process and their dignity around that process. Can you comment on that Mark?

Mark: The impact of lingering disease and death is very debilitating to one's concentration, one's spirit and one's power. You need all of your power. In a situation of a long lingering death, you have to consider the force of karma. This death came to you as your karma, thus it represents something that is seeking equilibrium in your life and so, as much as possible, you want to pay all your debts in this life before you move on to the next life. And if some of those produce a difficult setting, that's just a hard debt that came your way.

I believe in the use of drugs to decrease pain. It's not necessary that the person be in pain. It distorts the mind and it distorts the character in an unbelievable way and produces a level of mental exhaustion very quickly. I think death is an extremely personal process.

If you meditate every day of your life, it's not difficult to find how you are connected to the world and the process of Samadhi is really a reflex of the death process. You are drawing your life force into the shushumna and merging into the Great Light through the gateway at the crown of the head. Remember the first day of the (Joshua Tree) retreat we were talking about the tree of life. The roots of the tree are in the crown of the head and the fruit of the tree is the body and the process of the exit is just like a very deep and powerful meditation. So it's better when you are in that situation to simply organize yourself. By the time you get into those final conditions, you are in a full confrontation and communication with death. Death is not without mercy. It is best to exit a decayed body when there is really nothing to stay for. The body's been used, and it is diseased and wrecked. The fact is that the physical body is just the envelope. The subtle physical body is still perfect and so it's better to exit consciously. That can be done with the help of a spiritual teacher, a Guru or Shaman and your own prayers and connection to God.

It's not a matter of judgment. Suicide is not a judgment as in bad or good. It is only addressing the karmic weight of the situation and all karma must be accounted for. If you don't pay it in this life, it will follow you to the next. You might think that if this situation is so advanced now, why don't you just get this karmic bill over with and do the suffering you have to do and then leave. If you don't pay that karmic debt now, it's not like you can escape it. It will follow you. So it's very pragmatic in that way. If you have a connection to spiritual expertise, those kinds of situations can be greatly alleviated. Most certainly all responsible human beings should dedicate a solid portion of their lives to understanding life and thus they will understand their death.

This idea of life and death goes directly to the theme of the Joshua Tree retreat on power and the idea of embracing and coming into one's power. It is your power that dictates the terms of your life and dictates the terms of your death – directly and utterly so. The presence of power is the greatest and most wild-card factor of producing an improvement in your condition – improvement being defined by a minimal of suffering and the greatest amount of efficiency in spiritual work of each life.

* This transcription is offered at the feet of the Guru. While it has been lightly edited, every effort has been made to render it accurately as it was spoken. Please forgive any errors that may have been made in the process.

INDEX

A

accidental death 73, 224-225
actors 190-194
Alzheimers 131-132
awakening. *See* enlightenment

B

Bhagawan Nityananda 55, 218
Bodhicitta 8, 35-36, 46, 48, 52, 64-68, 73, 76, 80, 90, 111, 151-152, 159, 163, 207, 211-216
Bodhisattva 42, 81, 135, 176-179, 190
brain 10, 18, 19, 21-26, 32-34, 37, 40, 45, 63, 65-68, 73, 84-87, 90, 91, 111, 120, 131-132, 136, 152-154, 179, 190, 193, 209-213
  lizard 40, 85, 86, 91
burial 49

C

chakras 18, 21, 24, 34, 55, 59, 79, 134, 209-210
Chikhai 34, 39, 42, 54-56, 59, 63, 74-78, 101, 113, 151
Chöd 75, 135
Chonyid 34, 39-42, 55, 59, 61, 74, 76-93, 101, 153
colors 19, 20, 31, 49, 53, 55, 60, 81, 82, 89, 91, 94, 118, 159
connections 43, 101, 102, 132, 164, 177, 179, 188
continents 96-98
crown of the head 10, 18, 24, 32, 37, 48, 53, 66-77, 89, 149, 151-152, 159-161, 195, 208-213, 219, 229

D

Dalai Lama 14, 179, 199
day (also see illustrations 106-107)
  eighth day 80, 85, 88, 101
  eleventh day 89
  fifth day 82
  first day 80, 81, 137, 229
  fourteenth day 91
  fourth day 82, 192

    ninth day 88
    second day 81
    seventh day 84-87, 174, 219
    sixth day 82
    tenth day 89
    third day 81, 113, 122
    thirteenth day 91
    twelfth day 90
deities (peaceful/wrathful) 18-26, 34, 37, 40, 41, 43, 77-95, 111, 136-138, 153-155, 164-169, 175, 197, 209-210, 219-222
desire 23, 53, 69, 113, 153, 212, 224
dharma 1, 10, 12, 30-31, 34, 37, 45, 80, 90, 97, 143, 179, 189, 196
Dharmakaya 66,-67, 78-83, 102, 145
Don Juan 171
Dorje Chang 88
dream 4-5, 16, 20, 39-40, 54-62, 77-79, 87, 100-101, 131, 151-156, 161, 167, 170, 202-204
drugs 120, 229

E

ego 3, 138-139, 166, 168
    "I" 86, 138, 139
Elements 6, 19, 21, 29, 30-33, 40, 55, 59, 63, 74, 82-84, 118, 134, 148-149, 173, 205
    air 19, 30-33, 55, 60, 79, 82, 149
    earth 19, 226
    ether 19, 21, 30-33, 55, 60, 79, 82, 149
    fire 19, 21, 24, 30-33, 55, 60, 63, 68, 79-83, 149, 159, 160, 181, 210, 213, 223
    water 19, 21, 27, 30-33, 55, 60, 79, 82, 149, 181
enlightenment 1, 8, 19, 22-26, 35, 38, 43, 52, 55, 66, 71-77, 114, 134, 140-144, 157, 164, 176, 188, 190, 195, 211-215, 224
envy. *See* jealousy

F

fear 4, 8, 10-15, 38, 39, 54, 56, 86, 92, 162, 199, 200, 214
fibers 18-28, 32-45, 59, 65, 77-84, 90, 111, 117-119, 134, 153, 165, 195, 209-210

G

greed. *See* jealousy
Guru
    call on the Guru 77, 156, 201, 206
    grace 66-70, 88, 102, 127, 131, 142-143, 155, 201
    Guru's feet 145
    meditation on the Guru 99
    seat of the Guru 66-68, 72, 132, 133

H

Hell 57, 75, 81-84, 95, 115-119, 123, 137, 139, 166, 192
hospital 113

Hungry Ghost. *See* Preta

I

ida. *See* sushumna

J

jealousy 10, 11, 28, 29
Jesus 52, 114-115
Judgment 84-87, 92-93, 136-138, 148, 153-154, 168

K

karma 2, 15-33, 37-40, 49, 53-59, 74-87, 90-95, 101-102, 115, 126-138, 151-154, 164-167, 170-177, 184-195, 203, 218, 225-230
kerimas 91

L

lokas 84, 93

M

malini 90
medicine wheel 58
meditation 7-9, 16, 28-38, 45-48, 62-70, 83, 99, 143, 176-178, 195-199, 205, 211-216, 226, 229
Meher Baba 52, 146
Muktananda 160, 218

N

nine gates 33, 37, 59, 75 (also see Phowa)
Nirmanakaya 78
Nirvikalpa. *See* samadhi

O

OM 21-22, 33, 68, 78, 157
OM NAMAH SHIVAYA 21, 157

P

padma 89-90
Padmasambhava 1, 76
Paramahamsa Yogananda 169
phowa 61--77, 79, 86, 96, 100, 135, 142-143
pingala. *See* sushumna
prana 44, 46, 51, 141, 148, 222
Pratyahara 33, 66, 76
Preta 41, 75, 82, 83, 84, 95, 126, 127, 128, 130

R

rebirth 17, 29, 30, 34

S

samadhi 29-31, 38, 48, 49, 62, 70, 71, 133, 134, 147, 157-159, 199, 217, 227, 229
  Nirvikalpa 62, 64, 159, 160, 199
Samskara 11, 15, 21, 24
serpent. *See* kundalini
shaktipat 23-24, 27, 63, 66, 71, 126, 132, 141-144, 154, 155, 179, 184, 186
Shambogakaya 78
Shiva 19, 88-89
Siddha 133-134
Siddhaloka 72, 143
Sidpa 34, 41-42, 78, 101, 119
sitting upright 10, 45, 50-52, 56, 62, 84, 116, 125, 145, 152, 178, 226
six wheels. *See* chakras
sleep 30
SoHam 7-9, 35, 36, 73, 80, 118, 156, 157, 215, 222
sushumna 10, 18, 22, 24, 30-34, 45, 55, 59, 62- 70, 79, 118, 132-134, 152-154, 159, 205, 208, 213, 217, 227

T

three rivers. *See* sushumna
Tibetan 19, 121, 134-135
triangle 68, 132, 144 (also see illustration 105)

W

womb gate 42, 98-102, 135, 175-177, 221

Y

yellow fluid 49, 53

www.ingramcontent.com/pod-product-compliance
Lightning Source LLC
LaVergne TN
LVHW021659060526
838200LV00050B/2424